TRAVELS WITH MAURICE

An Outrageous Adventure in Europe, 1968

GARY ORLECK

Relax. Read. Repeat.

TRAVELS WITH MAURICE: An Outrageous Adventure in Europe, 1968
Gary Orleck
Published by TouchPoint Press
Brookland, AR 72417
www.touchpointpress.com

ISBN: 978-1-956851-10-6

Editor: Scott Baptista
Cover Design: ColbieMyles.com
Cover Photo: Courtesy of Gary Orleck

Visit the author's website at https://garyorleckauthor.wordpress.com

 @gorleck @gorleck

First Edition

Printed in the United States of America.

To all the people who rooted me on when the going got tough. They made me continue on my mission of telling the world the story that is so true no one could make it up!

Part I – In the Beginning

Prologue: 1998

I got the call at work and recognized Moritz's voice immediately from his German accent. His voice was thick with grief. He could barely get the words out.

"It's Maurice," he said. "He's gone."

Gone? As in dead? I couldn't seem to process the information. I stared blankly at the wall of my shop, specifically at a poster for Goodyear Tires. "How?" I managed to ask.

"Massive heart attack."

A heart attack? It seemed like such an unglamorous way to go, so incongruous with the enchanting no-holds-barred way Maurice had lived his life. I did the math in my head: he was only fifty-two.

I kept the call brief, and thanked Moritz. He was one of Maurice's other close friends from Munich, Germany and was clearly in a similar state of shock as I was. I hung up the phone a moment later.

I sat down in a chair and let the first wave of emotion wash over me. True, I hadn't seen him in years, but I still thought of him as my best friend. And now that cherished friend—the man who had opened the world up for me in ways I never imagined possible—was dead. Though nearly twenty-six years after the fact, I had to remind myself that the time we spent traveling around Europe just after college was not a dream, that I did not imagine Maurice. But in truth, I knew I had not. In the deepest depths of my mind, I could not have conjured up the times we had together.

I worked through the rest of the day in a daze. In my mind, I wasn't sitting in a tire shop in Rhode Island; I was driving along European highways with no speed limit. I was dancing in nightclubs in the South of France. I was dragging Maurice away from a roulette table at 3 a.m.

After I closed up shop, I knew I couldn't go home. I got in my car and drove ninety minutes to Boston. I found our old haunt, a bar called Flick's, whose motto was *"Where live wires connect."* Maurice had loved this place because it had an indoor swimming pool, like his favorite club La Siesta in Antibes, France. "It's not the South of France, but it's the closest thing I can find," he once told me. It felt right to be there, filled with so many memories.

After a few drinks, I climbed up onto the bar and stood there until the room was silent, with everyone looking at me. I asked the bartender to serve everyone a drink on me, and when everyone had their glass, I raised mine to make a toast to my friend and my brother. I thought of a toast Maurice had often made throughout Europe, and repeated the irreverent words, "Here's to those who wish us well, and all the rest may go to hell," I said. Everyone clinked their glasses and laughed.

It was a fitting send-off, but when I sunk back into my seat, I felt the acuteness of the loss. These people didn't know Maurice. Nobody had ever known him like I did: that devilish grin, those dark intense eyes, the way he entered a room and immediately captured everyone with his charm. The things he had shared with me on our drives across Europe were things I know for sure he had not shared with anyone else.

With that thought, my sadness dissipated for a moment, and a deep

3

feeling of appreciation for a friendship like no other filled me. Maurice was someone you might get to know once in a lifetime—if you were very lucky.

Now there was nothing left to do but to share his story with the world. What you are about to read is all true, every last word, as I remember it.

Chapter One

I first met Maurice at Babson College in Wellesley, Massachusetts. It was a traditional East Coast private school, the type where there are more trees than students. I was earning a business degree there and so was Maurice.

I actually heard about him before I ever laid eyes on him. There were whispers running through the school that a fabulously wealthy Iranian student had enrolled that year. Some people claimed he was a prince, a member of the Iranian royal family. Others said he was the son of an oil sheik, and that he lived in a palace with a tiger back home. One thing everyone agreed on was that he liked to gamble and could always be found at the local school poker game late at night, which was unusual for a student from Iran.

That's where I first saw him, hazed by the smoke and darkness of a college poker room. I played occasionally for a few dollars a hand, but, being a kid from Rhode Island whose father owned a Goodyear Tire and Auto Repair Shop, I knew I could quickly get in over my head. Maurice, however, looked like he belonged at that table—his dark hair was perfectly slicked back, his eyes darted from his very large pile of chips to the dealer's hand and back again. As he sat there grinning in his smart jacket, the way he carried himself made it look like any, or all, of the tall tales being told across campus might be true.

I only played a couple of hands of poker that night. The room was filled with smoke, and booze was being drunk by everyone. Maurice was on a hot streak and quickly cleaned me out of what few chips I had. He was polite, but serious about the game, and he wished me a cordial goodnight when I left the table. I left with more questions running through my mind about this mysterious Iranian man.

Despite the relatively small campus, I didn't run into Maurice again until months later. Thirteen guys, all from my graduating year, descended on Bermuda during the spring break of 1965. The holiday turned young men who had been relatively model citizens back on campus into creatures who only wanted women, alcohol, and sun—in that exact order.

Our leader, by popular demand, was Maurice. On the plane trip, he paid for three rounds of drinks for all the boys on board. Wherever Maurice went, the party followed. He had a magnetic quality about him that made you want to do whatever he said, not because you felt like you had to, but because you wanted to—for him and for yourself.

On the first evening of that year's spring break, Maurice set the precedent for the entire trip. He led us to a bar across the road from our hotel to have drinks while we waited for our scooters to be prepped for the rest of the trip. Maurice said the first round was on him, and a cheer erupted from our group. Once the drinks were no more, the group dispersed outside to wait for the scooters, leaving Maurice to pay the bill.

I thought it was rude how nobody had offered to buy Maurice a drink in return or even thanked him for all that he had done. I therefore took it upon myself to do so. I approached him while he stood at the bar, wallet in hand.

"Hey," I said. "I'm Gary."

"Yes, I know who you are, Garree," he replied. The last syllable of my name was so stretched out that it became like a long, protracted "ee" sound.

"Thanks for the round," I said. "Can I buy you a drink?"

A huge grin crossed his face. "Yes, thank you," he replied. "It's rare that someone offers to buy me a drink."

"What will it be?"

"Two bottles of Michelob beer?"

I signaled to the bartender and he popped the tops of two bottles. We clinked glasses and chatted for a short while. I learned that he was, in fact, from Iran but was not a member of the royal family, as some liked to claim. That said, I would later learn that his family's relationship with the Shah and with royalty in general was a lot more involved than he let on. Furthermore, he, like me, was studying business and hoped to start his own company someday. I wondered why he had chosen Babson when it seemed like he had the entire globe at his fingertips, but I didn't ask. Something about his short and indirect answers to all my questions felt evasive and protective. It was as if he were holding his cards close to his chest. After a few more minutes, a whoop went up from the boys outside. The scooters were ready.

"Time to go, Garree," Maurice said with a smile

I didn't know it then but offering Maurice that drink would end up changing my life forever.

Chapter Two

I returned to college after spring break and got on with my studies. As I was busy with classes and working part-time for the Goodyear Tire and Rubber Co. in Natick, Massachusetts, I didn't see much of Maurice over the next two years. After graduating from Babson in 1966, I spent the next summer working small, odd jobs as I made my way towards California driving Route 66. When I reached California, I spent about thirty days working at any Goodyear Tire and Rubber Co. store I could find in that state (an opportunity I was given access to because the regional manager of the Boston area knew my father well and connected me to the regional manager overseeing the western U.S.) before deciding to head back to Boston. I used a more northerly route to get back to Boston, and once I arrived in the city, I decided to move back in with my parents. Along with my earnings from the road and what I have saved up by working through college, moving in with my parents allowed me to save $3,000. I planned to use the money I had saved for a long trip as wanderlust was getting the best of me. I had seen the United States—now I wanted to see Europe.

Shortly after returning home on Labor Day weekend, my phone rang. It was one of my friends calling me in distress.

"My pocketbook has been stolen! My money, credit cards, and airplane ticket are gone, but I am supposed to go home for the long weekend! Can you please give me a ride to the airport? My parents got the ticket replaced, but I have no way to get to the airport."

The desperation in her voice made me feel really bad for her. Though I wanted to rest before ascending on the Boston nightlife, I reluctantly said, "Of course I will. What time?"

"Six in the evening would be perfect," she responded. "Meet me at my dorm."

"OK," I said and hung up. I arrived at her dorm five minutes to 6 p.m. and was waiting in the dorm's waiting room for her to come down. All of a sudden, I heard a yell from across the room.

"Garree!" shouted Maurice who came bounding over to talk with me. "Hi Garree! What are you doing here?"

"Just picking up a damsel in distress who had her pocketbook stolen and is desperately in need of a ride to the airport," I replied.

"That sounds like the Garree I was told about. Always the giver and never the taker," he replied with a grin on his face. "What have you been up to since we graduated?"

"I just got back from Route 66 where I worked my way around the U.S. for six months. It was a blast! This coming summer, I 'm going to do the same thing throughout Europe. Except, it will be more of a vacation."

"Great, me too! I'm going to spend the summer in Europe, so why don't we go together? I spent three years in Switzerland at a boarding school, three more in London at high school, and a bunch of summers in the South of France. I'd make a great tour guide!"

"Maurice," I responded. I did not want to hurt his feelings so I said, "There's no way I can join you since I cannot keep up with you—nor do I even want to try. I have three thousand dollars saved up and a roundtrip ticket so I am planning on only staying for as long as my money lasts."

I could see his mind working for a moment before he responded. "Garree, let's say that we each take three thousand dollars with us and when one of us goes broke, we'll both come back home."

I was taken aback as that not only sounded reasonable, but it also overcame my worst fear when it came to traveling with him. As such, I said, "Let me think about it."

"Meet me here at this dormitory next Saturday night and we'll go out to eat and discuss it. Please?" he asked. "I know you'll have the time of your life with me in Europe. I know that continent like I know the back of my hand, and I can show you places that tourists never see. Think about it."

By this time, two girls were there waiting on us. One of them was my friend, but I didn't recognize the other one. Maurice smiled at the woman I didn't recognize and introduced me to his date. I, in turn, introduced him to my friend. As we parted ways, Maurice turned towards me and yelled, "Bring a date, Garree!"

That night, my mind was spinning as I pondered what the future would bring. But no matter what I imagined, what actually transpired was far more fantastical. I was in Maurice's orbit now, feeling a gravitational pull toward an adventure that I don't think anyone could resist.

Chapter Three

That Saturday evening, my girlfriend Eileen and I met Maurice and his date outside the same dorm we had previously met.

"Garree," he said. "I'm so glad you came, and with such a beautiful woman. Please follow my car."

He and his very attractive date hopped into a sporty little Mercedes and sped off toward Boston. I followed in my Corvette—the only luxury I had. I loved cars, and this was "the car" of the time. I was so enamored with my car that I would not have traded "her" for a limo—or Maurice's Mercedes!

While on the way, we had to stop at a toll booth. I pulled up to the window of the booth after Maurice's car had gone through and was told that he had already paid for me. The same thing happened when I followed Maurice into the restaurant's parking lot. The attendant told me that my parking had already been paid for by the "gentleman in front."

Eileen seemed impressed by Maurice's generosity, but I didn't want his actions to go unrewarded. He had probably been running this routine on all his friends for years now. I wasn't going to let him get away with it this time. I had a plan.

Upon entering L'Espulier, a restaurant known for the finest French food in Boston, I pretended to go to the restroom. Once out of Maurice's line of sight, I went to the front desk and told them to make sure the check came to me. Feeling smug, I went to our table and joined the conversation with Maurice and our dates. The night was imbued with the sort of magic that only Maurice can spin as he told tales of gambling and nightclubbing in Monaco as well as charming anecdotes about how to get the best deal on a purse in Paris. Sometimes he talked about how he had three wives back home. At other times, he talked about how he was Empress Farah's brother and that his father was an oil sheik. We knew that it was all in good fun. Maurice, after all, had the gift of gab and charisma. He didn't need his wallet to charm the ladies.

Eileen spent the entire evening flirting with Maurice, but that was just fine by me. When we decided to call it a night, I gestured for the waiter to send over the check. He smiled at me and walked away in another direction. This reaction seemed odd to me, but I presumed he would be back soon.

Instead, a finely dressed gentleman walked over to our table and addressed me. "I see you've asked for the check?" He phrased it like a question, but it clearly was nothing of the sort. "Well, I'm very sorry sir, but this gentleman has prepaid with a signed check as he is a frequent customer," he said, waving his arm in Maurice's direction. "The check has been paid."

With a smile and a slight bow to Maurice and me, the finely dressed gentleman turned on his heels and walked away. Maurice flashed his all-knowing smile at me and said, "What can you do? I'm not a normal person, and I don't operate under normal rules. You will never beat me to a check." It was a challenge I promised myself would not remain true.

This event became the start of an ongoing competition to see who could pay first. The prize? Our pride. It was a fierce competition, one I realized would require me to use my wits to have any chance whatsoever of emerging victorious.

As the evening progressed, and we spent the next few minutes finishing our drinks and talking, I agreed to go to Europe with Maurice. The worst thing that could happen is that we wouldn't get along at some point, in which case we could go our separate ways. If Maurice wanted to "slum" it with me, that was his choice. When we left the restaurant, Maurice left a huge tip for the staff.

"Don't ever forget the little people, Garree," he said, smiling.

That sounded a bit arrogant to me, so I asked him, "What do you mean by 'the little people?'" Perhaps he considered me one of them! He took my question seriously, however.

"No Garree, he said, "I don't mean to belittle anyone. I know how much I have been given and how fortunate I am. I think it's important for those who have more, like you and I, to help people who do not have that behind them. I am just saying—be generous."

That evening had eased me into becoming more comfortable with Maurice's lifestyle. He did not show off but was just unashamedly himself. He was the most confident person, or at least the most-confident-*seeming* person, I had ever met.

We spent the next few months preparing for our trip while doing what we could to know each other better. We clicked and instantly became best friends, and even brothers during this time. He took me to the most expensive, fancy restaurants in the area, and I took him to the Hofbräuhaus House. This was where the likes of Peter, Paul, and Mary; the Kingston Trio; and Simon and Garfunkel all played to become famous. As it happened, going to the Hofbräuhaus got Maurice into enjoying American Folk Music. I tried my best to match his spending, but found it was impossible to do so. I needed to come up with a grand creative gesture to show him just how much of a "giver" I actually was.

I knew I could never match his lavish spending or impress him by taking him to a fancy restaurant as he had probably already eaten in all the ones located nearby at least half a dozen times. So instead, I invited him to spend a Friday night having dinner with me and my family. He'd told me that he had not had a home-cooked meal since leaving Iran about ten years ago, so I felt it was high time he got one.

He won my mother's heart almost immediately after entering the house by kissing her on the hand—European style. Pleasantries were exchanged, and before we knew it, it was time to eat. My mom cooked him leg of lamb, which she knew was a Middle Eastern favorite. She was greatly pleased when he gobbled it up with relish. Of course, my parents, who asked him to call them Charlotte and Bill, loved him immediately. Simply put, he was able to charm anybody he met, especially women of a certain age. That said, my father actually told me later on that he had never met anyone with his level of charisma and charm. Earlier that night, they had debated if it was harder to make a person's first million dollars or to double a person's first million. It was interesting to hear each of their sides, and though they held their own in the debate, they each respected the viewpoints of the other. Either way, if Maurice was able to make my *dad* like him in such a short time, he could work his magic on anybody. More importantly, his mannerisms and the expression on his face showed that he had appreciated the meal in a way that no fancy night out on the town could ever rival. He even told me that he felt the warmth of family again—something he was clearly craving. We asked him if he wanted to come again for more home-cooked meals and he emphatically agreed, managing to do so twice a month until we left. He never seemed to notice that my house was small or that we only had one bathroom. In fact, if anyone was self-conscious about it, it was me.

Until we left for Europe, Maurice and I spent weekends going to sporting events and enjoying other activities in the city of Boston. We attended Boston

Red Sox baseball games, Boston Celtics basketball games, and Boston Bruins hockey games. We also enjoyed sharing good meals together and going to comedy clubs to see some of the popular comedians of the day such as Rowan and Martin, Bill Cosby, etc. Though Maurice bought us the meals, I was the one to pay for the events.

Every time we met up, it was like entering a different, glittering new world. He was unique in every way which simply made me want to be around him and his attitude towards life even more. We continued to have dinner with my family every other Friday night. Due to this, my parent's house became a second home to him, as it was a place where he got to spend time with people who loved him and expected nothing from him. Maurice was one of those people who'd walk into a room and command attention naturally. It was mostly likely because of his confident posture, his good looks, and his storytelling skills. His smile and the twinkle in his eye let everyone know he was there to be the life of the party and have fun doing it. I think he deliberately made it his business to make me want to be his best friend—and he sure succeeded. More importantly, I never felt as though he judged me for living at home after college. Just the opposite, in fact. I think the fact that I lived with my parents showed him that I had a grasp on what truly mattered in life.

Whenever we spoke about our trip to Europe, Maurice was unworried about it. It was clear that his attitude reflected the "whatever happens, happens" mindset. Which was understandable as he had been traveling since grade school and had been on an unlimited budget for as long as he could remember. I was much more of a planner, and throughout the remaining time that we had in the U.S., I did meticulous research about where we would go, what hotels we would stay in, and what sights we would see. The detailed itinerary I drew up would begin with a visit to my uncle's farm in Ireland, before taking us on a path from London to Germany, Belgium, Amsterdam,

Scandinavia, Switzerland, Italy, Spain, parts of Eastern Europe, and France. My fingers trembled with excitement with every pen mark I made in the travel books I had previously purchased. Europe! It was not far off now, and I hardly dared imagine what awaited me on the other side of the Atlantic.

Before I knew it, my bags were packed and I was about to embark on the journey of a lifetime.

Part Two - Travels With Maurice

Chapter Four

Letting your Jewish mother finish packing your suitcase is never a good idea. Case in point, mine clearly thought I needed a lot more than I laid out the night before. Thank God airlines didn't weigh suitcases when you left America back in the 1960s, or I would have never been allowed on the plane. Eighty pounds of luggage later (double the weight it should have been), the majority of which would be lost along the road, I was finally ready to go to Europe.

We had a final goodbye dinner at a Chinese restaurant in Boston with Eileen and Robin, Maurice's girlfriend at the time. Eileen seemed a bit nervous to see me go but was reassured by the fact that she would be joining us in Majorca, Spain toward the end of our trip. "Don't worry," Maurice told her over dinner. "I will take good care of Garree."

"I see. Alright then," she said believing him, which wasn't much of a surprise at this point. Everyone seemed to believe Maurice. Anything and everything seemed possible when you were in his presence.

We were to leave for Ireland from New York City. Before we went to the Idlewild Airport (what is now the JFK International Airport), Maurice told me he wanted to say goodbye to his uncle John, who had an office in Midtown. This was my first introduction to Maurice's family, and I was excited. Apparently, Maurice had phoned his uncle ahead of time as a Rolls-Royce had been dispatched to pick us up at the airport. When we arrived in Midtown, I was dumbstruck for the office space was like nothing I had ever seen. It was elegant, opulent, and buzzing with activity. John—a man short of stature, but full of energy—greeted us with a handshake.

He took us into a room where there was a whiteboard eight feet above the floor that read:

NYC .86%, Goal 2%

Chicago .73%, Goal 2%

Miami .675%, Goal 2%

LA .91%, Goal 2%

SF .78%, Goal 2%

A crowd of employees read numbers off of four tickertape machines that churned out numbers.

All of a sudden, a wave of applause broke through the room.

"We just got confirmation that we purchased a shopping mall in San Francisco," John explained when he saw my confused face.

I watched in awe as an employee climbed a ladder and adjusted the percentage in the "SF" column.

"What does that mean?" I asked Maurice.

"It's the percentage of the city we own," Maurice replied.

"C'mon," John said. "Let's go have lunch."

He took us to Tavern on the Green, a place where people usually needed a reservation six months in advance to enter, and yet it seemed John had his own table ready and waiting for him. Over lunch, Maurice's uncle John opened up to me. He had taken on the American nickname 'John' in order to assimilate better in the New York City business world. Furthermore, when he was sent to New York City in 1936, the only thing he knew about this strange land was what he had learned from watching gangster movies at the cinemas back in Iran. Such movies featured James Cagney and Edward G. Robinson, stars who were iconic at the time. While looking for a home, he told the real estate agent that he wanted to feel safe, and to do so he would like to live near the famous mobster John Gotti. As it happened, he wound up buying the compound next door to Gotti.

"We see each other when we take out the trash," he told me.

While I was still absorbing this incredulous but true story, I saw that John had arranged for his Rolls-Royce to take us to the airport. As we climbed in, I thanked him profusely. This trip was already turning out to be spectacular.

We flew coach, which I could sense was not the norm for Maurice as his demeanor became stiffer. He decided to confess that everyone in his family always flew first class. Everyone, that is, except his father who always flew coach so as to remind himself where he came from.

During the flight, I excitedly explained my plans for the different cities we planned to visit. I spoke to him about various museums, squares, and famous churches. Maurice played along with me, smiling a bit of a knowing smile.

"Garree," he said after I had been speaking for nearly thirty minutes. "Let me tell you something. We are going to have fun on this trip. Fun can mean many things. It can mean museums and shops, but it can also mean girls and nightclubs. I have many things to show you."

"Oh really?" I asked, a bit incredulous.

"Don't worry, Garree," he said. "I will show you the ropes. I will be your tour guide so you can see what most people, most tourists, never see." He paused for a moment before continuing. "Maybe along the way I can help you build your confidence with women and become a little better storyteller.

Sounds good?"

"Definitely," I responded. I was happy to follow in his footsteps and ready for the unusual sights and fun he promised! Our first stop was Dublin, which was quiet and uneventful. We stayed on my uncle's farm a few miles outside of the city and slept on two cots in a barn. As you would expect, it was very cold and uncomfortable, but we took it in stride. We were young and strong at that time, after all. While in the area, we did some sightseeing, and some driving with a car my uncle kindly provided us with. The '60s weren't the best time to be sightseeing in Northern Ireland, given that the country was in the thick of The Troubles. During this time, Irish nationalists were fighting to get Northern Ireland to leave the United Kingdom and join a united Ireland. While we were there, we saw the British Army everywhere. We also frequently noticed tanks and armored cars cruising the streets, enforcing a nationwide 8 p.m. curfew.

Despite this, we made the best of our time there. The most memorable part of our time in Ireland was that we got to "kiss the Blarney Stone." Legend has it that kissing the stone brings you eloquence and persuasiveness, which helps bring women under your spell. Being typical young men, we both wished for this to help us with women. If the stories were true, however, Europe would seriously need to watch out, because Maurice already had these traits by the bucketful. I, on the other hand, was more timid. Given what I already experienced with Maurice before we left for Europe, I felt that the rest of the trip was not always going to be as placid as this first little jaunt on the Green Isle.

I recognized that Maurice was growing a bit restless, that he wanted to set himself loose on the continent. Of course, he was a perfect gentleman to my uncle, and never made me feel bad about the modest lodgings. No, that was not Maurice's way. But he couldn't hide the fact that he was intensely looking forward to our next stop—London. His sister Flora lived there, and

I could tell, given how much he talked about her and the city itself, that he had something spectacular in store for us.

Flora lived in a place that existed nowhere else in the world. She lived on The Street with No Name in a house with no number, which was one of, if not *the* most prestigious and desirable addresses in London. This avenue was home to ambassadors from all over the world, celebrities, and businessmen. "Posh," as the British would say. When we pulled up to the gate in a London cab, I was floored by the sheer size of her house. Mina, Flora's maid, answered the door for us and let us in. She would not let me carry my massively overweight suitcase, and instead, grabbed it herself before showing us to our rooms. The bedroom I was given was as large as my entire home back home. Mina then gave us a tour of the house. Room after room shone with opulence and good taste, with gorgeous paintings, shining marble counters, and lacquered wood floors.

"Your sister must be a successful woman," I told Maurice.

He waved his hand, as if this were all nothing. "Flora is smart," he said. "She owns a dress shop."

"Must be some dresses," I replied.

Flora was working at her dress shop when we arrived, so Maurice decided that we should immediately throw ourselves into the London nightlife. He told me to dress up in my best clothes as only black-tie would do. Unfortunately for me, 'black-tie' was not something I had packed, nor had I anticipated needing it on this trip. The best I could manage was black trousers and a white button-down shirt. Feeling a bit self-conscious about my lack of appropriate clothing, I set off with Maurice sensing that our trip had truly begun.

Maurice took us to The Revolution nightclub. If you visited The Revolution nightclub in the 1960s, it would not have been unusual for you to spy the likes of Elizabeth Taylor, Twiggy, or even Andy Warhol. Often bands of such caliber as The Beatles, The Rolling Stones, and The Who would play there. It has been said that playing a gig at The Revolution was the start of many high-profile music careers. It was the first of its kind. Before this, England had only pubs, which had no dance floors. In those places, people would just stand around drinking, oftentimes on the sidewalk, or "pavement" as they say across the pond.

When we arrived, the line was 250 people long with a wait time of two hours. In front of us, I saw women in gowns topped by exquisite fur coats and men in expensive suits with top hats and canes—fashionable gentlemen dressed to thrill. They waited around the block just to get in. What did we expect for the most exclusive club in London? I had never felt so underdressed in my whole life, nor have I felt so under-dressed since.

My heart sank when I saw the line. I was just about ready to turn around when Maurice strode off toward the great wooden door.

"Where are you going?" I called after him.

"Don't worry, Garree," he replied over his shoulder. "Just follow me."

I scrambled after him as he bypassed the street full of people waiting impatiently to get inside. With all eyes on him, he pounded his coffee-colored fist against the dark wood. A gentleman opened the peep hole and asked Maurice, rather brashly, what he wanted. Maurice puffed out his already broad chest and exclaimed, "You tell David Shamoon that Maurice Elghanayan is here!"

Barely a minute later, a voice over the club's loudspeaker invited Maurice's "party" to the front door. The door swung wide open, and we were immediately surrounded by an opulence of red velvet and gold finishes. The sheer volume of people within the walls of the club made it seem as though the club was living and breathing. A stage, a dance floor, a restaurant, a casino; there was something for everybody and for every taste.

Mere moments after we entered, we were shown to a table on the front row, smack-bang at the center of the stage. Waiting for us were two bottles of the finest champagne I have ever seen. At this point I knew I was out of my depth. I took in my surroundings and sank into a chair. Turning to Maurice, I asked, "Okay, tell me. How did you do this?"

He looked at me, a sly grin on his face. Sipping champagne, he replied, "Garree, it's a long story. I'll tell you the short version." Maurice had this way of captivating people. He was able to monologue and leave people in awe of the story he was telling. Though it's a bit difficult to explain, it was basically the way he spoke. When listening, you would feel like he was letting you in on his biggest secret.

"My sister Flora came over here from Iran over twelve years ago to open a boutique," Maurice began, gesturing in the general direction of her house. "She ate at the restaurant next to her boutique all the time. She came to know the people there well. One day, she noticed a handsome gentleman looking at her from across the room. Their eyes kept meeting. Eventually, Flora decided to go over and start a conversation. The man introduced himself as David Shamoon. He told Flora that he'd come to London from Iraq to make his own way in life after being disowned by his father for not wanting to go into the family business. His father, as it turned out, was an unbelievably rich man, owning the bottling rights to Coca-Cola for the whole of Egypt, amongst many other things. He did business in various countries and really embodied the definition of a tycoon. Essentially, there was "rich" and then there was him. David Shamoon told Flora that his dream was to open nightclubs in London. He wanted an *empire* of nightclubs for the rich and famous and decided that London was the best place to start because there were only pubs there."

I took a long sip of the delicious champagne, which we drank from delicate crystal flute glasses, and leaned forward on the table, captivated.

"Flora left the table and asked to borrow a large satellite phone from the owner," Maurice continued. "She went outside and made a call to our dad in Iran. When she returned to the table, she looked David Shamoon in the eye and told him that she wanted to make him a deal: one hundred thousand dollars for a fifty percent share of his business. She wanted to be equal partners. You see, Flora realized how right David Shamoon was about London only having pubs when they met. He agreed, shook her hand, and that was that. She then took out the rather large satellite phone she'd borrowed, placed a call, and the next day he had a cashier's check for one hundred thousand dollars. She only borrowed the money from our father because he could get it to her faster than her own bank; her husband would have had to cosign for a withdrawal of that size. It was a loan not a gift, and I know for a fact that she paid it back within a week. Flora and David have been partners for over ten years now and own twelve establishments, including the best-known casino in England, The Grosvenor Casino. That's why they let me in when I told them who I was."

As if on cue, the aforementioned David Shamoon sauntered up to the table with three gorgeous women—a redhead, a blonde, and a brunette—draped over him like stunning pieces of jewelry. The women gazed around the room languidly, an air of indifference coming from them like a smokescreen. They were clearly used to the atmosphere and used to the attention. I, however, probably had my jaw on the floor. All of this was new to me—cutting a line at a popular nightclub which your sister had funded and co-owns.

"Maurice!" David exclaimed, shedding his lovely hangers-on and giving my friend a big hug. "It's been too long." Looking at me, he asked, "Who is your friend?"

Maurice introduced me to the six-foot tall, well-dressed man and filled David in on our plans to drive around Europe. I was still completely awestruck. The owner of the club stood at my table, and Maurice was chatting with him as though this was a completely normal occurrence. Of course, as I was starting to learn that this *was* normal for Maurice.

David assured us that we could have any drinks we wished, as well as any food we wished. He wanted us to have a good time there. More specifically, he wanted *Maurice* to have a good time there. You see, David knew that Maurice could put on a show, and easily become the life of the party. He made men want to be him, and women want to be *with* him. David knew that anybody who set eyes on Maurice would have a good time, and that would help his club to prosper. Before he left the table, David passed Maurice a £500 chip and a pair of keys. "Go put on a show," he told Maurice. "Later, feel free to use my penthouse if you want. It has a bar, one hell of a view, and a new round bed," he said, winking at us before swaggering away. "By the way, if you see any celebrities or women you want to meet, including the Rolling Stones, anybody, I will handle that."

"C'mon, Garree," Maurice said. "It's show time."

I barely had time to grab the still full bottle of champagne and follow him to the gambling rooms. Tables full of seated men and women stretched out around us, undoubtedly betting untold amounts of money with dealers in tuxedos taking their chips. Maurice stood in front of a roulette wheel and bet his £500 chip on a single roll. He won immediately.

"You see, Garree," he said. "You have to play to win."

Within minutes, Maurice had a crowd of onlookers watching him play. And boy was it a roller coaster ride. At first, he was up by about £5,000, and then he was down £1,000, then back up £10,000. The crowd rode the waves with him. Raucous cheering erupted when he was winning, and intense silence spilled over the room when he was losing. Nobody could play a room like Maurice. After the first dozen rolls, I returned to our table and watched from a distance while I ate my steak, drank my champagne, and tried to let this insane night sink in.

Almost an hour later, Maurice came back to our table, his arms laden with chips.

"How much did you win?" I asked.

"Not as much as I'm going to," he replied. There was a look in his eye that I had never seen before.

"Follow me," he instructed.

I followed him up to the top floor of the building. We arrived at a huge double door with an armed guard stationed at each side. I expected the guards to question us, but they let us walk straight by, into a private room. The room was stark and only had a circular poker table at its center, with a small bar area in the far corner. Six men sat at the table, hunched over their cards. They were all sweating excessively, their faces various shades of red.

We walked silently over to the bar and perched on the stools that were half hidden in the shadows of the room. Maurice bent over to me and whispered, "There's one million dollars sitting on the table. Have you ever seen this much cash in your life?" he asked. As he explained, each hand could be worth anywhere from $25,000 to $100,000. As it was a cash game, the mountain of money dominated the table. Can you, dear reader, imagine seeing that amount of money in pound notes piled up on the table right in front of your eyes? Believe me, it's an astonishing sight.

My head, already swimming from the champagne and the dream-like quality of the evening, began to whirl. I could never imagine having that much money in the first place, but to *gamble* that amount was unthinkable. These men belonged to another class: the ultra-rich. They lived in a different world than the rest of us, with different rules.

"They must be crazy rich," I told Maurice.

"They are helping to make my sister rich," Maurice replied, studying the game. "Two percent of each pot goes straight to the club. She makes anywhere between £500 and £5,000 per hand."

Sipping another glass of champagne that Maurice had placed into my hand, I couldn't take my eyes off of these men. The tension in the room was like nothing else. Every move they made was deliberate—every yawn, every sigh, every sip of a drink. I was watching something very few people would ever have the chance to see. I turned to Maurice to express this sentiment, but he had vanished.

Looking around the room, I couldn't see him anywhere and suddenly felt very out of place in this high roller's room. Maurice's presence allowed me to pass into these milieus unquestioned. Once he was gone, I felt exposed as the tire shop kid from Rhode Island that I was. I slipped out and went looking for Maurice. I found him in the casino surrounded, once again, by a crowd engrossed in his roulette streak. I gave him a wave, went back to our table, and had another couple of glasses of champagne. Maurice returned to our table about an hour later, a giant grin on his face.

"Garree, I ended up losing it all," he said.

"Well, you certainly put on a show," I replied.

"Always, Garree."

"It was just five hundred pounds."

"Sure, Garree. Sure."

As both of us were unsteady on our feet from enjoying the very expensive champagne throughout the night, Maurice decided to find David's chauffeur to take us back to Flora's. When a Rolls-Royce pulled up, I was hardly surprised. At this point in time, anything and everything seemed possible to me.

As I stumbled out of the Rolls-Royce and up the stairs to Flora's front door sometime later, I felt like I was floating, high on the night's events and beyond excited for the rest of our trip. If our first night in London was like this, I couldn't wait to see how the rest of our travels would unfold.

Chapter Five

The next day I met Flora and immediately became smitten with her. She was unlike any woman I had ever seen before. She had the same honey-colored skin tone as Maurice but even darker eyes. Mahogany hair flowed around her shoulders and fell to just above her waist. Flora was older, worldlier, and completely unattainable. Despite all this, we fell into easy conversation. She offered to take me shopping, as my wardrobe was what could possibly be described as "unfashionable."

"Should we wait for Maurice?" I asked.

"Was he out gambling last night?" Flora asked, arching an eyebrow.

I nodded.

"Then we have a few more hours till he's up and running," she replied with a smirk. "Come, let *me* show you London."

I obviously acquiesced, and we soon after set off into the city. Walking around the teeming Oxford Street and Piccadilly Circus with Flora was an experience in itself. She held herself with such confidence that the crowds on the streets parted for her.

As we walked around London, Flora told me about her wedding in Iran.

It was a magnificent affair, with fruit flown in from Lebanon and flowers from Switzerland, all amounting to the royal sum of roughly $1 million. She laughed about how her father had paid a $100,000 bribe in order to get one of her uncles' out of prison for the day to attend the wedding. But when she talked about her husband, I could see regret enter her eyes. On this subject, and this subject alone, her confidence seemed limited.

I was so grateful for Flora's company when we went shopping. She took me to one of her favorite menswear stores, and I ended up with some more appropriate attire for my evenings out with Maurice. When it came to paying the bill, I got out my little money clip, but Flora waved her hand at me.

"Maurice has an account at this shop. It's already been added to his tab," she said.

"Flora, I can't . . ." I began.

"Please," she said, "he was the one who told me to take you shopping. And he's going to pay for it. But I do get a deep discount so no worries. It's nothing. Besides, you need to look the part if you are going to be his partner in crime."

Later in the afternoon, Flora showed me her boutique, a gorgeously appointed shop on one of London's most exclusive avenues. That said, Flora's boutique was more like an art gallery. The clothes that she chose to sell in her store were works of art, the finest satins and silks from all over the world—an explosion of color and class.

"Look around. See if anything takes your fancy," she said.

My eyes searched the walls, landing on a gown that I knew my mother would love. Its intricate emerald beading on a deep green bodice would make her look like a queen. I was staring at the beautiful object when a commotion interrupted the tranquil scene.

A man had backed his Mercedes up to the front of Flora's boutique, blocking anybody else from entering the store as well as the entire sidewalk.

He had started shouting for Flora to bring out his packages. Eight large, wrapped packages, each with NO CUSTOMS/DIPLOMATIC IMMUNITY scrawled across them in bright red marker, were soon brought to his car by one of Flora's employees.

Flora rolled her eyes. "It's the Iranian ambassador," she explained. "He's a frequent courier for the princess and a bit of a pain."

The ambassador then stormed into the store, gesticulating like a mad puppet. He was supposed to take *nine* packages back to Princess Farah Pahlavi, then the Empress of Iran, but there was only eight brought to his car. Flora explained to him that one of the dresses was not quite finished and would be shipped when it was up to the princess's standards. Due to the fearful expression that flashed across his face, he was clearly terrified to go back with less than nine packages. She told him she had already telegrammed the princess regarding this. The ambassador unwillingly accepted this explanation, jumped in his car, and screeched away. The smell of burnt rubber filled the air and lingered there for a moment.

"Ambassadors! What can you do?" Flora said to me, laughing.

A short while later, we met up with Maurice for lunch at a quaint glass-fronted café next door to Flora's shop. It was her favorite haunt.

"Did you help Garree find some nice things to wear?" Maurice asked.

"Yes. I think he'll fit in a bit more now," Flora replied.

After the check came, we were surprised by a commotion taking place on the street outside. A huge group of people crowded around a cherry-red 1968 Cadillac convertible, a rare sight in the U.K. The car's long body and the crazy amounts of chrome paint made it stick out like a sore thumb. Flora leaned towards me and said, "I always wanted a Cadillac, you know? Especially this model."

"Elvis had a similar model," I replied.

She asked if, once back in the States, I would be able to procure this exact model on her behalf. Unsure of whether or not she was joking, I explained that it would cost nearly $20,000 to buy one and get it shipped to her in England.

"No problem," Flora said, grinning. Just so you know, dear readers, $20,000 in the '60s is the equivalent to about $150,000 nowadays. Once again, I felt as though I had stepped into another world—a world where money was no object, and anything was possible. The feeling was incredible. I never wanted it to end.

Chapter Six

The next day, Maurice and I used a London taxi cab to get to a dry dock where we waited to pick up one of Flora's cars, which we would be borrowing for the remainder of our trip. Our plan was to then head to the Ferry Port of Dover and catch a boat to Antwerp, Belgium.

On our way to the dry dock, we stopped off in Dover to see Maurice's younger sister, Sharit, whose "American" name was Shirley. We decided to take Sharit, who was at a boarding school in the area, out for lunch at a lovely little coastal café. While Maurice was eating, staring at a young leggy blonde in the corner, and simultaneously chatting with his sister, I snuck off to pay the bill. Though he never talked to me about what I did, by the expression on his face, I could tell that he was pleasantly surprised that I beat him to the bill. Moreover, his sister was too, and the story made it all the way to Tehran to Maurice's father. This, of course, was not known to me at the time, but Sharit rang her father from her school that evening and told him, "Dad, Garree beat Maurice to paying the bill today! I've never seen Maurice so happy. It's like he's finally got the brother he's always wanted."

It turned out that Flora had told her father something similar—that I was good for Maurice and that I pulled my weight, which his other friends never had. It would have been nice to know what Flora and Sharit said at the time, but Maurice was a very proud person. Either way, I would have loved to have been able to read him as well as both his sisters could.

Once we had used a London taxi to drop Sharit off at her school, we continued on our journey to pick up our new mode of transport. Prior to leaving America, Maurice had explained to me that the cherry-red Mustang we would be driving for most of our trip was unregistered. The license plate and registration documents deliberately did not match as this would allow Flora to avoid the exorbitant tax placed on foreign cars entering the country. Knowing this made me nervous, but it didn't seem to affect Maurice in the slightest. It was just something that his family did to make life easier and save them some money. While speaking to Maurice about the subject, I learned that due to this same entry tax, renting a car in France that wasn't made in the country was also extremely expensive. Unless you wanted to drive around in a Peugeot, that is, and Flora didn't strike me as the type. Maurice had also explained to me that this practice was actually quite common.

Before we left the U.S., I had already decided that since Maurice wasn't going to act upon the mismatched documents, *I* needed to. I didn't want to drive for months worrying about possibly getting pulled over with a faulty registration. As such, I went to a junkyard in Rhode Island and got a set of used but decent-looking license plates. Then I hightailed it down to the registration office, got a blank form and filled it in with the new information, forging the registrar's signature as I went. Until this point of my life, forging the registrar's signature was the boldest thing I had ever done. Though we had only spent about a year together at that point, Maurice was already beginning to have an influence on me! Flora had used this car purely for when she went to Europe, so it was easy to get a green card for insurance. As such, all I needed to do was pack the plates and documents in my already overflowing luggage.

The shiny red American Ford Mustang with a dark black roof we picked up that day stood out in the street like a sore thumb. I opened the hood as soon as I could to inspect it, but by doing so I became the closest body to the driver's side. Maurice then swiftly yelled for me to drive so I reluctantly closed the hood and prepared myself to drive the beautiful machine. Now, I'm ashamed to say this, but I struggled to start the car to drive it to the port. My driving experience was vastly limited back then, and the 1967 Mustang had a tricky anti-theft device, that I sometimes tripped.

"Come on, Garree, drive!" Maurice said, laughing, as we lurched down the London streets. "We have a ship to catch!"

I finally figured out the Mustang's idiosyncrasies after a little bit and managed to get it to the dock. Unfortunately, there was no ship there to meet us. Standing at the edge of the water, looking out to sea, we could just see it disappearing into the distance. Panic instantly struck me when I realized what had happened. I didn't want to waste any of our trip, and as such, I wanted us to be on our way to Belgium, as we should have been. I racked my brain to think of a solution. Nothing. At this point I turned to Maurice to ask if he had a plan and realized that he wasn't there. As he had a habit of disappearing while I was lost in thought, I wasn't that surprised.

Scanning the port, I saw him about fifty yards away at a phone booth. He was leaning against the glass of the booth, totally nonchalant, speaking into the receiver. After about thirty seconds, he meandered his way back over to me. "Don't worry, Garree," Maurice said.

"When is the next ship?" I asked, still a ball of nerves.

"I have no idea," Maurice said.

"Well then who the hell were you calling?" I asked.

"Just watch," Maurice said.

He pointed out to sea, and I watched in disbelief as the ship slowly turned around and made its way back to shore. I looked at Maurice in confusion. He had a smug look on his face, as though he had just achieved the impossible. Which, by the way, he had.

"Did you know, Garree," he said. "That in England, you can make a call from the dock to a ship if it's less than five miles away?"

"Maurice, what did you tell them?"

"I simply told the captain that I'm Princess Soraya's brother, and that I'm supposed to be meeting her in Belgium shortly. That if I were to miss my boat, the princess would be most unhappy."

I shook my head in disbelief at his cheek, but also at his confidence. Princess Soraya was very much loved in Europe at the time, a real celebrity. She had been the Shah of Iran's most beloved wife. That said, they were, unfortunately, unable to produce an heir to the throne. And so, with great regret, the Shah had needed to find another wife who would be able to fulfill this duty. Princess Soraya therefore found herself rich, and inopportunely without a husband. As a result, she spent all her time, and money, helping children from many European countries by opening hospitals and orphanages. She was treasured by everybody. Maurice had decided to use this knowledge to his advantage, as only Maurice could.

When the ship docked, four uniformed men in full three-piece black suits and white gloves disembarked. They introduced themselves to us as the captain's staff and told us they had been sent to help us get our car onto the ship. They then went to the car, put it in neutral, took the handbrake off, and pushed it up the ramp and into the cargo hold of the ship.

Once aboard, we were escorted to the captain's quarters for shrimp cocktails and champagne. Maurice engaged the captain in deep conversation, while I smiled and nodded when asked a direct question, trying to comprehend what had just happened. It was like being in the midst of a movie. I kept asking myself, *Will the wonders never cease?* While we were enjoying our lunch with the captain, somebody on the boat checked out the car and realized that the steering wheel had to be positioned at its dead center for the car to start—a real crazy anti-theft set up which had caused me some trouble earlier. This was explained to us which allowed us to avoid a lot of future problems. We were also given an overnight cabin right next to the captain's. It was certainly nice being with "Princess Soraya's brother."

After an overnight trip, we docked in Antwerp, Belgium. We then quickly drove off toward Brussels and to the Hilton Hotel where mail was waiting for us. This was another one of Maurice's tricks he taught me while traveling. In order to make sure you get your mail (at least in the '60s), you can have it posted (with a note saying: HOLD TILL ARRIVAL) to any fancy hotel that you pass on your travels. When you pass by the hotel, you would simply stop in and ask for your mail, saying that you had planned to stay at the hotel, but met some local friends which will be providing you with room and board. That said, these hotels would only hold mail for ninety days.

Please note that our mail stayed in the finest hotels in Europe, even if we didn't always. Once at the Hilton, we noticed news trucks, reporters, and hundreds of people blocking our entry. We parked the car on the street and fought our way through the crowd, before I discovered the longest red carpet I had ever seen. It ran from the pavement and ended about fifty feet or so from the front desk of the hotel. I tried to avoid stepping on the immaculate carpet, but Maurice, in typical Maurice fashion, had the audacity to stroll straight down the middle to the front desk.

At the front desk, the attendant efficiently retrieved our mail from the cubicles in the back. Maurice had apparently already asked for our mail before I got close to the front desk and was speaking to someone else. I said thank you to the attendant and prepared myself to leave. Before I could turn away, however, I realized that Maurice was still speaking to a man behind the counter. I managed to catch the end of the conversation. "There must be some mistake, I have a reservation. I'm supposed to meet my sister Soraya here this weekend," Maurice said.

The attendant looked worried. "There must have been a mistake," he said. "Soraya is not coming until next weekend. But if you wish, a room can be arranged for you. At a discounted price, of course."

"That will be fine, thank you," Maurice said. "Good man. Could we get a bite to eat?"

"No, the restaurant is closed."

"Oh, why is that?"

"The King and Queen of Belgium are now dining with the King and Queen of Denmark," the attendant replied. "They were filmed by television cameras for some kind of public announcement."

"Could one of your staff give a note to the royal diners, asking if it would be acceptable if Soraya's brother and his acquaintance could dine in the restaurant?"

"Sir, the restaurant is closed to the public."

"I know, but will you please just send the note?"

"Very well, sir."

According to Maurice's note, we had just had a "grueling" journey from England and needed a simple meal. It was agreed that we could dine there, so long as we ate in the far corner of the restaurant. The royals sent over a bottle of champagne, and I insisted that we simply raise our glasses to them, as I couldn't imagine disrupting a royal meal. Maurice was very disappointed, however, as he wanted to go and thank them personally. Thank God he listened to me! I didn't know how long he could keep the charade going. We ate quickly and went up to our suite of rooms.

At this point of our trip, my mind was simply reeling. We had stayed in the most prestigious part of London, turned a ship around, and dined in the same room as royalty. What had I gotten myself into? I was nervous about impersonating royalty with Maurice and playing what could become a dangerous game. But I also knew I was never going to back out. I had gotten a taste of something that I could never have back home. It wasn't the money, the champagne, or the lavish food. It was living your life exactly the way you wanted to at any moment. I had a taste of *freedom*. Maurice was, in fact, showing me what it was like to really live, unencumbered by everyday worries.

As I lay in that luxurious hotel bed later that night, my heart beating out of my chest, I truly felt free for the first time in my life. It was like being reborn. This time, into a shiny world of possibility and adventure.

Chapter Seven

The next stop of our trip was Amsterdam, unquestionably one of the most beautiful cities in the world. After settling into our hotel, we decided to take a stroll beside the Amstel River. As Maurice caught the eye of every young lady who walked past, I began to think that this was pretty much how I had envisioned our trip panning out. As we walked along the water park of the North Sea canals, spotting the rainbow of houses, as well as the colorful people, everything felt normal for a change.

We settled into the ebb and flow of the city, visiting museums, gardens, taking bicycle rides, and partaking in the "cannabis culture" of the '60s. I'd almost forgotten that Maurice led a life very different to my own until, after a night of heavy clubbing, he suggested we go to the Red-Light District. I acquiesced and joined him as he made his way there. This district, for the uninitiated, is a part of Amsterdam where there is a high concentration of ladies of the night. They sell their wares from large, glass windows of a single bedroom apartment, silhouetted against the stark backgrounds, their bodies lit up and displayed by the red glow of the lamp by their windows. The lamp would be turned off if the ladies of the night were not available. The streets were extremely narrow, with tall buildings lining either side, and women of all different body types flirting with both men and women as they passed by. Maurice made his choice in a matter of minutes: a beautiful blonde with legs for days.

I, on the other hand, spent the rest of the evening wandering around the maze of streets, too picky or too nervous to make a decision. With over two hundred choices, I didn't even know where to begin. Well, in truth, there was more to it than that. I had never slept with a prostitute and didn't know how I felt about it from a moral standpoint. I wasn't convinced that it was *wrong* per se, but I also wasn't ready to hop into bed with a strange woman I also had to pay. I was still green in that respect compared to Maurice, but I also wasn't ashamed of that fact.

The next day, Maurice and I decided to split up and each do our own thing. I had more than an inkling as to where Maurice was headed. For me, I decided that since we were supposedly connected to Princess Soraya, the great helper of children, I should visit an orphanage and volunteer for the day. I did some research and found that one of the orphanages she had funded was right here in Amsterdam.

I envisioned myself walking up to an imposing Gothic stone structure, something out of a Charles Dickens novel. However, when I arrived, I found out that what I had imagined could have not been further from the truth. The orphanage was modern, having been built only a few years before. Without having to lie about anything, I got permission from one of the caretakers to take some of the children out to a nearby park to play, so long as a few of the nuns that helped run the orphanage came along with them. I bought them all sweets and ice creams during the excursion, including the two nuns who accompanied us. To this day, it was the best money I have ever spent. After spending time with the children, the feeling that I was left with was beyond anything I'd felt before. This is what I'd hoped that traveling would be like. Although I knew that traveling with Maurice had its rare charms, I also knew it would afford me precious few moments like this one.

When I met up with Maurice at the hotel that night, it was clear that we'd had very different afternoons. To his credit, he listened to me while I told him all about the orphanage. He even became a little emotional.

"Always thinking of others," he said. "That's why you're one in a million, Garree."

"All I did was buy a few ice creams."

"It's not about how much you spent," Maurice said. "It's never about that."

Before leaving Amsterdam, we ended up spending one afternoon watching the Grand Prix. I loved being around cars, but the smell of gas and oil, as well as the deafening noise of the race was not what Maurice would call "ideal." Given that I had pit passes provided to me by Goodyear, Maurice spent most of the time talking to the very attractive girls found in the pit area, most of whom were the girlfriends of the drivers.

Amsterdam would be the first and last place I felt like a normal tourist. After this, Maurice came into his own, and the trip became one hell of a wild ride.

If I'm being honest with myself, I'm glad that it did.

Chapter Eight

The next stop of our trip was Paris. The city of romance, culture, and art. As it turned out, this would not be the relaxing tourist stop I had anticipated. Paris was going to become a unique adventure all to itself. Driving into the city, we saw armed troops everywhere. They were crawling over the streets like insects. Every time we turned a corner, we were greeted by a sea of camouflage. We parked the car and walked into the throng of people to investigate. Maurice was always one to get into the thick of things so there was no keeping him away from the unfolding drama.

After asking dozens of people, we finally found one person who spoke English well enough to explain what was happening. Students all over France were rioting. They were protesting against the "oppressive social norms" of the time. Paris, so it would seem, was the epicenter of the protest—and of the violence.

Years later, the riots all over the country (and especially the riot in Paris) were credited with pushing France into its current era and way of thinking. At the time, however, it was frightening. Riot police formed barricades to prevent the students from doing too much damage. The students retaliated with force, and there were quite a few casualties. Martial law was declared shortly after we arrived. As such, no one could enter or leave the city. Moreover, the hotels in the area had been taken over by local people who could not leave Paris after work. People we met on the street and various hotel attendants told us that there was not a hotel room to be had anywhere in the city.

"What are we going to do?" I asked Maurice.

Maurice looked at me, smiled, and said his signature phrase, "Don't worry, Garree."

With that, he walked off into the crowd. I followed at his heels, eager to see how he could possibly get us out of this situation. He eventually stopped in front of the Ritz-Carlton, at the time the most expensive hotel in Paris. Of course, the first thing we did was pick up our mail. After that, Maurice addressed the hotel receptionist and asked, with absolute confidence, "Are there any rooms available?"

"Sir, the only room available is the Queen's suite."

"The rate?"

"One thousand two hundred dollars a night."

"Maurice . . ." I nervously cautioned.

"Don't worry, Garree."

Maurice asked the clerk if he could use the phone and called someone. He spoke quickly and then handed the phone back to the clerk, who nodded. To my absolute shock, we were handed the keys to the Queen's suite a moment later.

As we walked to our room, my shoes sinking into the plush red carpet, I couldn't help but stare at Maurice. He walked around like he owned the place. When he threw open the double doors to our room, his reaction was the exact opposite of mine. He seemed to drink it all in. My jaw, on the other hand, hit the floor.

For a boy from Rhode Island, what I saw was to me, unimaginable. This suite was bigger than the house I grew up in, and the closet was bigger than my two-car garage back home. It had two gigantic master bedrooms, with suites and bathtubs the size of cars. I had also never seen so much fabric in my whole life. It draped every surface, making the room appear like a palace. Maurice walked the length of the living area, over to the table where an ornate bowl of fresh fruit sat alongside a bottle of champagne. He picked up an apple, took a bite of it, poured himself a glass of champagne, and sank into one of the sofas. With an apple in one hand, and a champagne flute in the other, he exhaled a deep breath and shot a pleased grin my way.

I wish I could have been able to relax like Maurice, but I couldn't see how in the hell we were going to afford this room. I had just $1,800 left to spend. Maurice, had much less than me. I turned to Maurice, still relaxing on the plush velvet sofa, and asked how much all this had cost.

"Nothing," he replied, his eyes fixed on mine, gauging my reaction. I walked over to the window, took a deep breath, and braced myself against the polished wood of the sill.

"How in the world do you figure that?" was all I could choke out, my mind trying to reach for possible explanations, and failing miserably.

Maurice strolled over to the window and put his arm around my shoulders, his apple still in hand. "We are now guests of the Shah of Iran's current wife and his sister," he said, as if this provided adequate explanation. When I didn't respond, he continued, "They are here on a shopping trip, and Flora is here to advise them. She's actually staying right next door."

My ears pricked up at the mention of Flora. Although it had only been a matter of days since I had last seen her in London, I wanted to see her again.

My good mood only lasted a few minutes as it began to dawn on me just how low we were on money. I didn't want to freeload off of other people, especially Flora, but I also didn't want to cut our trip short. I decided it would be best to mention my concerns to Maurice. I only had $1,800 left, and we still had half of our trip left. It took me a little while to build up the courage to speak to him about this since I didn't want to cause any arguments. In the meantime, we made our way to our own bedrooms, showered, and relaxed for a bit.

I finally approached Maurice in his private bedroom a couple of hours later. He was getting changed, readying himself to go out for the night. Looking at him, it dawned on me how different we were in appearance. Where he was angular and sharp, I was slightly softer. My mousy brown hair was cropped much shorter than his, which he wore at almost shoulder length. I'm not saying I wasn't good looking; I know that I was, but in a very different way—a more approachable way. Girls looked at Maurice and saw a challenge. Girls looked at me and saw a possible husband.

While all these thoughts were rattling around in my head, Maurice turned to look at me. "Everything okay, Garree?" He spoke the words slowly, like he could tell something was wrong.

"Not exactly, Maurice," I said.

"What's wrong?"

"Look, with the budget we agreed on, I can't afford to stay in places like this. I don't want to sponge off your family. And I know you are also getting low on funds."

"Ah, Garree, that is what you are worried about?"

"Yes, it is."

"Well, it was not my intention to ask my sister for help. I had originally planned to find our own hotel, but due to the unfortunate circumstances we find ourselves in, we were unable to do this. Flora was our only means of finding somewhere to stay. You can't control a riot, Garree."

"I suppose you are right."

"I wanted to ask Flora for help even less than you. We won't do it again."

Who could argue with that? I questioned why I had ever doubted him. That said, I was still worried. "But Maurice, this still doesn't solve our money problems for the rest of the trip."

"Don't worry. I have a plan."

"Oh yeah, what's your plan?"

He smirked at me and continued, "Right after Paris, I'm going to send a telegram to my dad. The same one I always send." He chuckled to himself. "It goes like this: 'Dear Dad. No mon. No fun. Your son.' To which I always get the same response: 'Dear Son. Too bad. So sad. Your Dad.'"

"How on earth does that save you?"

"It's a little joke we have. He always sends me the money."

"Well, that doesn't solve *my* issue."

Maurice must have read my face pretty accurately because he lowered his voice, looked straight into my eyes and whispered, "You have a bit of money left over. I promise you, that after Paris, I will sort this out. I will get my money, and we'll be rocking and rolling again. Your money will last, I promise you."

And you know what? *I believed him.* It was astounding, but he had the power to sell sand to the Saharans. Besides, some part of me knew that no matter how guilty I felt, or how broke I got, I would never leave this trip. How could I? Already more had happened to me here than in a lifetime at Babson, or at my father's shop. With Maurice by my side, we would make it—even with the riots of Paris.

"Okay," I said. "I believe you. But just promise me one more thing."

"What's that?"

"No more asking Flora for anything."

"I promise. But if she offers you something, it's impolite not to take it. There is a difference between asking for something and accepting a gift."

"That's true," I said.

47

The next day, we lunched with Flora. God, I had missed that woman. She was such a breath of fresh air and being in her presence simply made me feel happy. That said, she was also just like her brother in many ways. For instance, they both had an easy nature, as well as a nonchalant way they moved through the world. I tried to get the check so I could pay for lunch but found out that the meal was automatically charged to Flora's room. As we left the restaurant, she threw a huge tip on the table.

"My father says to always remember the little people, Garree," she said, winking at me.

That afternoon, Flora invited Maurice and me to high tea with the Shah's new wife, Empress Farah. I dressed in one of my new outfits, a velvet blue suit and matching bright-colored tie, which Flora had helped me pick out in London. Maurice, as usual, was fashionably dressed in a black shirt and white sports coat. Once ready, we made our way to meet Empress Farah, her sister, and Flora.

When we arrived, I was astounded. The hallway to their room was wide enough to fly a small plane through. Moreover, if our room was nice, theirs was a literal palace, the very height of luxury. Upon entering, I addressed the ladies of the room, saying "Salamat" by way of greeting. I always like to learn some basic phrases from the countries I intend to visit. I also wanted to impress the Empress as I was absolutely floored by her beauty. She had shoulder length hair, and I could tell she had one of Flora's beautiful creations on. That said, it was her smile and dark brown eyes that caught my attention. To me, she was far more lovely than most actresses.

Presuming I spoke Persian, Empress Farah chatted away to Maurice and Flora. I smiled and nodded politely at various intervals so as not to be rude. I did manage to catch that Maurice said I owned the Goodyear Tire & Rubber Company, a billion-dollar company at the time. He had said the company's name in English so I started to deduce that they were talking about me and my family. My father, however, only owned a single Goodyear Tire store so I was not too happy about what I overheard. Simply put, I did not, and still do not like misleading people.

When I confronted Maurice about it later, he said that he wanted me to be treated with the same respect as they treated him. He said he was looking out for me. He wanted the Empress and her sister to perceive me as an equal. He explained that though I didn't need to be seen as rich for my own self-worth, in some situations, such as being in the presence of an actual princess, being perceived as rich just made it easier to function. I had not been living this way before, as Maurice clearly had, so if he insisted that he was looking out for me, it made sense to follow his lead.

When Empress Farah directed a question directly to me in rapid Persian, I realized that I had to come clean about knowing very little of the language. Thankfully, she found it funny and Maurice translated the rest of the conversation. Empress Farah explained, through Maurice, that she was impressed that I had taken the time to learn a few words in their language. Maurice explained to her that I was interested in learning about Iran. Since this was during a time when 99% of Americans could not point out Iran on a map, the Empress was keen to discuss her country with me. With Maurice's help, we talked about Iran for an hour. She was very proud of her country and excited to be able to educate somebody about its rich and turbulent history. I'm proud to say that I held my own by knowing the history of the Persian Empire and the Pahlavi Dynasty. She was really impressed by my knowledge, along with my interest about her country. We got on so well, in fact, that Maurice and I were invited to visit the Shah of Iran in Monte Carlo in the near future, an incredibly exciting possibility. She also mentioned that the Shah loved automobiles and "would love to hear about your drag racing experiences."

All five of us chatted away until late in the evening, laughing at each other's stories, and sipping tea. It was so relaxing that I couldn't believe I was dining with royalty for the second time in less than a week. This road trip just kept getting more and more surreal. That said, as the night wore one, I started becoming uptight again.

Later that evening, Maurice and I decided to go out drinking to blow off some steam, and boy, did I need it. The combination of royals and money troubles had made me a bit uptight. Paris was still under martial law, but we managed to find some places to get drunk and have fun. We danced with some beautiful women and had a wonderful time as we moved from club to club.

When it was time to go back to the hotel, Maurice found our Mustang and jumped into the driver's seat. I got into the passenger seat, and we sped off a moment later. Unfortunately, as we turned down the Avenue des Champs-Élysées, I realized that I really needed to urinate. All the alcohol had caught up with me, but the city was still in lockdown, and it was very early morning. That said, the road was completely vacant and there was no one in sight.

"Maurice, stop the car. I've got to go," I yelled into the night.

"No, no, Garree. I'll just slow down. Climb up on the hood and go off the side of the car."

"I can't do that. I'll be shot by a soldier!"

"I'll tell them we have diplomatic immunity."

"Maurice come on, stop the car."

"Just do it, Garree!"

The next thing I knew, I was standing on the hood of the Mustang, taking a piss in the middle of The Avenue des Champs-Élysées. Maurice, laughing his head off, started driving the car toward the Arc de Triomphe. As crazy as this night was, I needed it. I needed a bit of normality, away from the money and expensive hotel suites. It grounded me for the rest of our trip. While the royals and the rioters alike slumbered, Maurice and I pulled dumb schoolboy antics in the middle of the night in Paris, laughing all the way. Who else would pee on one of the most famous and well-known streets in the world?

Chapter Nine

After saying goodbye to Flora and thanking her profusely, Maurice and I set off for Denmark. Knowing that we were heading to the land of the midnight sun—and blonde women with slightly looser morals—made us eager to get on the road.

Our route took us through Germany, which we went through as fast as we could, stopping only for food and gas for the Mustang. Considering its history, and the fact that we were both Jewish men, Maurice and I did not feel comfortable spending more time than necessary there. It was 1968, not terribly long since World War II. That said, the twelve-hour drive, our longest by far, seemed to go in a flash. The roads were quick and smooth, and I managed to top 120 miles per hour in the Mustang. It was an exciting experience. We talked and laughed the entire way, sharing stories about our pasts and our wishes for the future.

Maurice asked about my life back home. I obliged and told him about my family, my dreams, and my dad's store. The more I spoke about myself, the more I wondered about Maurice. As I said before, he usually kept his cards very close to his chest. You only knew what he wanted you to, and never any more. As such, it made me feel incredibly special when he began to open up about his upbringing as we drove through Germany. Perhaps it was because we were two Jews traveling through a country that had such a horrible history with people like us, that we were able to connect on that drive in a way we hadn't before.

It was on that drive that Maurice told me, for the first time, how he ended up going to college in the U.S. Keeping his eyes on the road, he spoke slowly and deliberately. He explained, "The last time I went home was in 1963 so as to ask my dad, face to face, for money so I could attend a university in the U.S. Though I had gone to high school in London, after I turned eighteen, if I ever went back home again, I would have to do two years mandatory service in the Iranian Army. I told my dad I wanted to speak to him about something important, so he asked me to meet him at the casino at what was called the Babolsar Hotel for supper."

"Why ask you to meet him at the casino?" I questioned.

"This was part of his routine, Garree. After working all day helping people with their problems, he would have supper at the casino. Every night. When I met up with him, I told him that I wanted to go to college in the U.S. He stopped eating his food, put down his knife and fork, and looked me in the eyes. He asked me how long I would be there for and I told him it would take four years for me to get a business degree. His face never changed, not once. He's a very hard man to read, my father. He picked up his pen and wrote one million two hundred dollars on a napkin and told me to give it to my uncle in New York City."

Maurice paused to take a breath and then continued. "He explained that that amount of money would help me in my endeavors, but that he wanted something in return. As it turned out, he wanted me to be up at 6 a.m. the next morning, dressed and ready to go on a ride. He then explained that upon returning, he wanted me to meet him for one final supper before I left. So, obviously, I got up the next morning and waited on the steps in front of his house. Did I tell you about his house, Garree? Designed to resemble the Casino Monte Carlo and built especially for my dad."

Maurice paused for a second before continuing. "Anyway, early the next morning one of his staff members named Imran picked me up in a black Bentley. I got into the back and Imran explained that we were going to take a ride around my dad's estate, or as much of it as we can before the day ends. One million acres, Garree. My dad has over one million acres of land!"

Maurice sighed for a moment. "I didn't return home until eight that night," he said as he continued. "When I went to meet my dad at the casino, he asked me how my day went, and I replied 'long.' Then, Garree, he told me this while grinning,

'Son, I wanted you to realize before you leave that the land you saw today is all ours. There are opportunities for you when you return. Have a good time in America. You have a lot to look forward to when you get back.'

So, Garree, when you ask me what I'm going to do with my life, the answer is that I don't know. I will always be in my father's shadow. If I took two hundred men and stood them one on top of the other and then climbed on their shoulders, this would still not cast a shadow as long as my father's. Nor do I want to enter into a race I cannot win. I'm still figuring it all out, Garree. And look at what we've got ahead of us."

The road unwound in front of the car, the sun beginning to set on the horizon. For the first time ever, I began to feel as though I knew Maurice. I began to see the truth behind the confident act he displayed to the rest of the world. The wealth that was at his fingertips was unimaginable, but so was the responsibility. There was a cost to all the money, all the finery. Maurice had to be his father's son. There was no other option.

I thought about the pressure I felt from my own father to take over his tire shop and realized that it was nothing in comparison to what Maurice went through on a daily basis. At some level I was glad that I didn't live in his particular corner of the universe. At least I could be my own man, unburdened by the trappings of an empire.

As we reached the border of Denmark, Maurice grew silent, even a bit moody. Perhaps talking about himself so much in a way he was not accustomed to had made him turn inward. The border crossing was crowded with guards, most of them carrying rifles. Since our car was unregistered, we had to be polite, inconspicuous, and respectful at the borders of all the countries we crossed. However, for reasons unknown to me, Maurice started mouthing off to the officials. We ended up having our car pulled over and searched. This was the last thing we needed. I was on edge but tried to stay polite. I thought my good attitude would compensate for Maurice's poor one that day. During the search, I spent an hour physically keeping Maurice away from the officials, while he muttered curse words under his breath in at least two different languages. The stern officials searched every inch of our car, and even dismantled our spare tire. It took over an hour and I'm sure they were angry that they didn't find anything. It could have been my imagination, but their faces seemed awfully red when they had to put the car back together again. All in all, we arrived in Copenhagen an hour later than planned, feeling the pressure from our close call at Border Control.

Due to the delay at the border, we had trouble finding a hotel room. Unsure of what to do, we began asking around among the locals to see if anyone knew of good hotels in the area that might have a vacancy. As luck would have it, one local recommended that we try a ship called the St. Lawrence, which previously sailed from Canada to Europe and was now dry-docked in Copenhagen. This turned out to be a fabulous decision. The boat had been turned into a hotel and had its own nightclub onboard, which provided us with endless entertainment in the evenings throughout our week-long stay in Denmark.

On the second day in the country, Maurice and I went to visit the Tivoli Gardens. The gardens had breathtaking displays of flowers, dancing fountains, foods from all over the world, and even some rides. In the evenings, everything in the park was lit up. Fairy lights hung from every building, the fountains glowed from within, and streetlamps illuminated the pathways

We spent three evenings there, with Maurice flirting with the ladies as usual. Throughout that time, all I could think about was that I would love to bring someone special here in the future. This place had such a magical energy to it that it just felt right that you should be there with someone you love. It is rumored that Walt Disney agreed with me, as some people suggest that after visiting this park, he patterned much of Disneyland on it.

I felt extremely lucky to have found the Hotel St. Lawrence and the Tivoli Gardens while in Denmark, but I also got lucky in another way. Over the course of our friendship, I witnessed Maurice meet and woo women with ease. For me, it was slightly more difficult. I didn't think I was bad looking, but Maurice had this utter confidence about him. He could go up to anyone, prince or pauper, and literally charm the pants off of them. He'd tell the most bizarre stories to women, and they would believe him. You always believed Maurice. He often told people that I was a Texan millionaire and he'd been hired to show me around, or that he was an escaped Persian slave. "Yes, they still have slaves in Persia," he'd say, with the most serious look on his face. However, my favorite story of Maurice's involved turtles. Yes, you read that right. Turtles.

It normally went something like this: a couple of young women would be sitting in a bar. Any bar, it doesn't matter. It always went down the same way. Maurice would stroll up to them and take a seat on a barstool, not too close as to be intimidating, but close enough that they knew he was there. I was usually at his side, trying not to draw too much attention to myself. He would smile at them, that typical Maurice grin, and ask to buy the two "lovely ladies" a drink. I'm telling you; no one could resist that smile.

The ladies let Maurice buy them drinks. Then, before they would get a chance to speak, he would launch into the turtle story. "Well ladies, I'm in these parts because I'm in the turtle business. You ladies know anything about the turtle business?" Of course, the ladies smiled and shook their heads, usually giggling to themselves. "Well, I don't really like to brag about it, but it's very lucrative, and has me traveling all over the world. My job is to procure the highest-grade turtles and sell them to NYC bars. The bars would then have turtle races which create an avenue for betting and drinking. The turtle who loses then becomes turtle soup, which everyone loves. Anyway, I'm away from home a lot, and it can be very lonely." Maurice usually deployed his "puppy dog eyes" at this point. "How would you like to keep a lonely turtle salesman company tonight?"

Anyway, the story he used on the night I got "lucky" wasn't this one. In fact, it could be argued that this new story was even less believable. It all started when he strolled over to a redhead at a bar in Copenhagen. It was a small bar, mostly full of young men and women traveling the world. I lost him to this redhead within minutes of our stepping foot into the bar's dingy, poorly lit entrance. I followed and sat a couple of barstools away so as to not disrupt his verbal flow. Then I heard him say, ". . . an oil prince from Persia. I have three wives already, but none as beautiful as you. You are something else." His accent was suddenly ten times stronger. Familiar with the ending of this story, that his brother had four wives already so he needed to find his fourth wife, I turned my attention elsewhere. I had learned from Maurice that you don't have to be the most handsome man in the room to end up with a gorgeous woman, but you do have to be confident and interesting—and quite possibly the funniest.

Taking heed of what I had learned, I turned to a lady sitting next to me. She was dressed all in black and had the palest blonde hair, which fell straight to her hips. When I asked her if she would like a drink, I noticed her piercing pale blue eyes and (I'm sorry if you think I'm being crude) her mountainous breasts stuffed into her corset top. I did all I could to keep my eyes focused on her face. It was gently lined which revealed that she was older than me.

Before I could stop myself, I started with the turtle salesman story, and we ended up talking and laughing for hours. I was thanking my lucky stars that I had listened to Maurice when she began hinting that she would like to come home with me. She caught me off guard, however, when she said that if I would like her to join me for the evening, she must go and tell her *husband*, who was in a club across the street. Apparently, open marriages were fashionable at that time in Denmark. While she was informing her husband of our plans, I told Maurice that I would be leaving and taking the car. He didn't mind as, with a wink, he told me he didn't think he would be going to our hotel room that night. Slapping me on the shoulder he said, "You're one in a million Garree. Go have some fun!" The elongated "ee" sound resonated in my head as I noticed that the redhead from earlier was obviously keen on the "oil prince from Persia," as she was still hanging on his every word.

The blonde and I, whose name I hadn't yet managed to catch, made our way back to the Hotel St. Lawrence. Who knew it would be so difficult to drive with a woman such as this sitting so close, though not touching? Sexual tension filled the car like a thick fog. We parked the car and made our way back to my hotel room, still not touching each other in the slightest. As soon as the door closed behind us, her hands were all over me, and I was pushed back against the door. It didn't take long before our clothes were scattered all over the floor and we were under the covers. Without going into too many details, it was a night I would never forget. She taught me things that have come in very handy in my future romantic relationships. God bless that woman. God bless Denmark.

The following day, Maurice and I deliberated on where to go next. We ended up spending the next few nights in Norway, and did much the same things as we did in Denmark, clubbing, eating out, etc. Not only was the atmosphere in Denmark more alive, but the women—at least the ones we met—were far more fun. Maurice and I agreed we liked Denmark more. As proof that we were right, every young person we met in Norway desired only to spend time in Copenhagen, like we had just done. We decided afterwards to not backtrack through Denmark and Sweden to get to Finland. We looked into visiting Russia, but we found that Maurice, as an Iranian, could not enter without a visa. As such, our next thought was focused on Germany. Although we both had some reservations, again due to us both being Jewish, we decided to push through our anxieties and see what it had to offer us.

Chapter Ten

The Autobahn, the German highway system, had no speed limit when we drove through it (nor does it now, I might add), so we finally got to test the limits of the Mustang. The guttural rumble of the engine was the soundtrack to our drive as Maurice continued to open up to me with things only his close family knew. I listened to him intently and noticed that whenever he talked of things that he clearly told no one else, he stared at the road, and rarely blinked.

"Did I ever tell you about when I decided Iran wasn't for me?" Maurice asked, as I piloted the Mustang.

"No, Maurice."

"Well, my dad always hired many builders for construction jobs. Once one of the men ended up at the emergency room. He'd stepped on a rusty nail. This actually kept happening. The workers would remove wooden panels and beams full of old nails and throw them 'nail up' onto the ground behind them. They didn't seem to learn their lesson."

Maurice paused for a moment before continuing. "At some point in time, I got fed up and decided to speak to the workers myself. I got them all together and explained, in their own language no less, that they needed to place the boards' nails down. I even demonstrated this. I walked away that day feeling accomplished. The next day, however, the workers were back to their old habits, visiting the hospital regularly for shots because they kept standing on rusty nails. That was when I decided Iran wasn't the country for me, because the average person is too stupid to think for themselves." He turned towards me and laughed, an incredible belly laugh, and I found myself joining in. Only Maurice could take something so trivial and base an entire life decision around it, but that was Maurice. He was able to be decisive in ways that I simply could not be.

"You must have a complicated relationship with Iran," I said.

"Garree, you don't know the half of it."

"So, tell me a quarter of it. We have time."

"There is so much corruption in Iran. If the Shah wants something done, let's say he wants to build a road for example, he calls up his friend and advisor and asks how much it would be to do this. His advisor then calls his friend, who works in construction. The construction worker quotes ten million dollars. The advisor calls back the Shah and says it will cost fifteen million. Not a bad paycheck for a ten-minute phone call, eh Garree?"

"Not bad at all."

"This is just one example. You could apply this philosophy to everything that is going on in Iran. Somebody is always being cheated." Maurice sighed and continued, "The Shah is not a bad man, Garree. I wouldn't want you to think that. But try as he might, he is not capable of running the country." He paused here, trying to find the right words to continue. Lost in thought, he stopped his monologue and stared out at the countryside as we zipped by fields of cows, pastures, and farmhouses.

"Maurice?" I asked, softly to bring him back into the present without startling him.

He looked at me for a couple of seconds. I could almost see a fog clearing from behind his eyes. "Sorry, Garree," he responded, blinking.

"Where did you just go, buddy?"

"Oh, you know, I was thinking about somewhere far away."

"You were telling me about the Shah," I reminded him. But some part of me continued to wonder what he had been thinking of as he stared off into space.

"My family knows that the Shah is a weak leader, as do a lot of the intelligentsia in Iran. They try not to acknowledge it. They do not want to accept that he may fail as the king of our country. In such a turbulent time, a weak king could cripple Iran. His head is mostly in the clouds. He simply never had a 'normal' life and thus knows nothing of the problems facing the poor in my country. You'll never believe this, Garree, but for his eighth birthday he asked his dad, the previous Shah of Iran, for a bat and a baseball after having watched a baseball game on satellite TV. The next day he was given a solid gold bat and ball that nobody could play with. It is because of this that I know he does not walk among us. He does not know what reality is."

"Many of *our* leaders are the same way."

"No, not like this," Maurice said. "It is a different world. He's a womanizer and a gambler, and he can afford to be. He cares deeply for his country, but he cannot run it. Period. He likes to be surrounded by 'yes-men' who will cater to his every whim. He plays King but only makes superficial decisions for the country. Anything more involved, and his advisors make the decisions. He has a man in Savak, their brand of CIA, whom he relies on greatly for important decisions. This man is both brutal and corrupt. He is a despicable human being."

Maurice rolled down the car window and spat into the wind, a look of disgust painted on his face. "Power corrupts, and absolute power corrupts absolutely. Remember that? Do you understand now why I have such conflicted feelings about my country?"

I nodded slowly, trying to absorb the information Maurice had shared. Iran was corrupt. I understood that. The Shah was a good man, but a bad leader. I understood that too. What seemed to hit me the most was that I was one of very few Americans who now had such an insider's understanding of Iran. The way Maurice talked about it so stoically scared me. It was just to be accepted that his country was like this and that you couldn't do anything about it. Yet another lesson, that things are not always as they initially appear to be, and that people can apparently put up with or overlook at lot

"What was it like it to grow up there?" I asked. "You seemed to be close to the action."

"We grew up almost next door to the Shah. I know him well. He holds my father in very high esteem, not because of his wealth, but because of his brain. The Shah believes my father can see into the future. His luck in business is beyond that of any other person in Iran."

"Is it difficult to be a Jew in Iran?" I asked, knowing full well the history of the country, and the history of the roads on which we currently drove.

"It can be, certainly, but my father has helped make things better for *our* people. A third of the royal guards are Jewish because my father told the Shah that Jews would lay their lives down for him. The Shah is good to them. He gives them freedom with no persecution. He trusts my father so wholeheartedly that their taxes aren't worked out the official way, like everyone else's. The royal tax collector comes to my father with a figure of how much tax is needed to 'balance the government's budget' and this is what my father pays."

Maurice said these incredible statements in a matter-of-fact manner, just like any other story one would tell of their next-door neighbors.

"That doesn't seem like the process my father goes through to pay his taxes," I said. "He's always complaining about the IRS."

"Things work differently in Iran. I remember a time when they tried to overthrow the Shah. I was probably ten. American and British foreign agents tried to strip the Shah of his power and make Iran democratic." At this point Maurice let out a low laugh, as if that concept was ridiculous.

"What happened?" I asked, literally on the edge of my seat as the Mustang flew around a tight curve.

"The Shah fled the country. He wasn't worried about his people—he was worried about his treasures. His palace was full of gold, priceless antiques, paintings, and government papers. When the Shah got wind of the coming trouble, he arranged to have this royal treasury hidden in my father's attic, of all the places in the world. I was awakened one night by the royal guards, 200 of them, marching up the stairs, carrying these priceless royal treasures. To a Jews' attic where no one would think to look! Soon enough, the Shah was back in power, with all of his possessions surrounding him."

"Tell me something else I might not know about your dad."

Maurice pauses for a second, mulling over what he should say. "I am not saying my dad is a secret asset of the Mossad, but he might know a guy or two there, if you catch my drift. My father is really good at getting money delivered to where it is needed."

"How does that work?"

"Well, Eli Cohen, the greatest spy to ever live, was undercover for years in Syria as a wealthy playboy. My dad moved money through the Israeli Diamond Exchange, which he owned, to him. My dad could get money moved all over the world without anyone realizing it."

"Wow, Eli Cohen, huh?"

"When the Mossad needed funding in unfriendly countries, they went to my dad. They paid him, and then he got the money safely to where they needed it to be."

"Your dad sounds like an amazing man."

"My dad was requested by the Shah to visit Russia as his economic advisor. Not only did he open up a lot more trade between the two countries, but he also came home owning 5% of the only palladium mine in the world."

"That is one of the rarest minerals on Earth," I said.

"If my dad fell into a pile of horseshit, he would come out with a gold horseshoe in his hand. When the Shah called him in to congratulate him, my father wanted something in return. He wanted to build a secret pipeline to Israel at his own expense in order to deliver lifesaving oil at a fair market price. The Shah agreed, an act that took some guts as he would have been assassinated if the Arab world had found out. My father built one third of the pipeline and then stopped the project. He told everyone that the family company went bankrupt to throw people off and help keep the project a secret. He would then reopen the project with a new crew for the second phase and did the same for the third. It was all kept under wraps. My dad never got any credit for this, yet Israel could not have survived as a country because at that time, no one in the world would sell them oil. You could consider him a secret agent for sure, Garree," he said to me proudly.

"Tell me something else about your parents."

"Well, after they had been married for five years, they decided to form a new tradition—an annual trip to Europe. On the first trip, my mom took five empty suitcases for presents. You see, Iran did not really produce anything, so she shopped for the entire family during that trip. Normally, they would just walk through customs, and their luggage would be loaded on a truck and delivered to their home. This continued for thirty-five years, and each year she added a few more. On their fortieth year of being married, my mom informed my father that she would be taking one hundred suitcases to Europe that year."

"What did he say?"

"He tried to tell her that it was far too many, but she wouldn't listen. So, he set something up to teach her a lesson. When they returned from Europe four weeks later, my mom was brought into the Customs office alone, while my father walked into passport control. The officials—who were in on it with my dad—started going through the suitcases one by one, adding up the taxes owed on the imported goods. My mom went berserk, yelling at them, 'Do you know who I am?' One of the officials could see her getting red in the face, so he went to find my father. When my father got to the Customs office, he found my mother nearly on the verge of a major meltdown. She has just been told that she owed fifty-six thousand dollars in taxes, and if she didn't pay it, she would have to go to jail. He quickly escorted my mother out of there, fearing she would collapse from anger. He told her, 'Don't worry, we will just pay a flat tax, like always.'"

"I bet she was happy about that."

"Oh, Garree, she didn't speak to my father for thirty days. The silence was deafening. But, the next year, when he asked her how many suitcases she was bringing, she replied, 'Is twenty-five too many, dear?'"

I looked at Maurice's profile in awe as he drove. I knew his stories were real, but dear God, they were unbelievable. I truly believed Maurice had opened up to no one else in quite the same way as he did with me during this long drive through Germany. This belief made me feel like I was stealing a seat in some of the halls of power and influence in which Maurice had lived his entire life. I turned to look at the road again as I contemplated what I heard.

"Look," I said, pointing to a mile marker. "We've almost reached Munich."

"That's good, Garree," Maurice said. "I must be boring you with my stories."

"The furthest thing from it," I replied earnestly.

"I'm excited to see Moritz," Maurice said, referring to his German friend, an old high school roommate who was putting us up.

"Me too. And if Munich is anything like everywhere else, we'll have a good time," I said.

"We'll have a good time because we are together, Garree," Maurice said, smiling at the horizon.

Chapter Eleven

The fact that we had arrived in Munich was signaled by the blur of trees shifting into large grey buildings. We approached Moritz's house in the early evening, with the red sun descending low into the sky, encasing the heavy stone building in shadows. Moritz stood waiting for us near his gate. Upon seeing Moritz, I immediately noticed how much his appearance contrasted with that of myself and Maurice. I had thought Maurice and I looked extremely different, but we could have been twins beside Moritz. He had white-blonde hair and the fairest complexion I'd ever seen.

"Ah Maurice," he greeted us, "Welcome to Germany."

"Moritz!" Maurice said, all charm and wiggling eyebrows. "I am here to get you into some trouble."

"Oh, I know you are! And you must be the famous Garree," Moritz said, shaking my hand.

"Guilty as charged."

"Well come in, come in," Moritz said. "You've had a long drive."

Staying with Moritz and his family, I learned a lot about European hospitality. His mother and father, both sets of grandparents, and his brother's family all lived in this house, and each and every one of them welcomed us with open arms. The house itself, however, was much larger on the inside than it had appeared from the outside. When Moritz saw the confusion on my face, he explained to me that the house was what the European's call a "terraced house," meaning that it was attached to other houses in a long row. In this instance, the row of houses snaked far into the distance.

Moritz had to attend school through the week, so Maurice and I planned a visit to the former Dachau Concentration Camp. Given our heritage, we felt this was important to do. Driving up to the camp gave me a horrible feeling. The first thing I noticed as I walked up to the iron gates with Maurice, was that the air felt thicker there. I was filled with a sense of foreboding and I felt almost lightheaded, as if the oxygen had been sucked out of the atmosphere. We shared a look, both experiencing the same sensation of dread as we continued on through the gates.

We spent that entire day at Dachau, eager to learn everything we could about the camp. At Dachau, we visited a barracks and crematorium, along with the showers and ovens, all kept in the exact condition in which they were found. For us, as for many people of Jewish heritage, as perhaps it should be for everyone, it was a rite of passage to know as much as we could about the atrocities, and about all of the lives that ended there. Though Maurice told me it was just my imagination when I told him about it, I swear I could smell human flesh decaying and see it hanging on the barb wire fences. Interestingly, Maurice had an equally strong but different reaction. He seemed removed, retreating into himself. We did experience things differently in general—I was prone to a visceral reaction; Maurice was always more guarded. In either case, the experience of visiting a place like this never leaves you. It is something I often think back on, and when I do, all those feelings of sadness, anger, and fear come rushing straight back.

As we left, Maurice turned to me and said, "I think something like this could happen to the Jews of Iran."

I nodded sadly.

Both of us were still in quiet contemplation when we stepped through the old wooden door of Mortiz's home. It was a Friday evening, which is the start of Shabbat in the Jewish religion and meant that the family was rather busy. Sabbat, the Jewish Sabbath, begins at sundown on Friday and lasts till sundown on Saturday, which is the Jewish day of rest. Moritz's father was a very strict Jew, which meant that every week, his family followed this tradition.

Sitting down for Friday night dinner with the family was just perfect for me as it was the only home cooked family meal we had had in our ten weeks of traveling. This return to normalcy put me at ease. There were so many people seated around the table that the atmosphere was buzzing. The children, Moritz's nieces and nephews, laughed all the way through dinner, then fell asleep in their chairs as the night wore on, their faces glowing in the candlelight. The rest of the family, however, was merry from the rich red wine that had been flowing.

When the food and wine was finished, Moritz's dad retired to the living room, gesturing for Maurice and me to follow him. Maurice declined politely, preferring to rest in his room and read the Holocaust books he had purchased at Dachau that day. I, however, followed Moritz's father into the living room and watched as he sat in a plush burgundy wingback chair, illuminated only by the candles on the table next to him. He gestured at the identical chair next to him and I sat down, sinking into it. We sat in silence, tumblers of whiskey in hand, until Moritz entered the room. He perched on the arm of his father's chair and addressed me, "I'm here to help him tell his story. His English isn't so good."

His father started talking while Moritz assisted with difficult translations.

His voice was gruff, had a strong German accent, and never wavered. Moritz's father was an incredibly brave man. This is the story he told, in his own words.

"When that madman came to power, my family tried to stay out of sight. To be invisible. It was easier said than done. That bastard, that Hitler, had ways and means of finding people. We could not leave our home. I *would* not. My business was here, my family. I believed that the German people would be civilized, that they wouldn't turn on us. Eventually, we were taken to Dachau which was only ten minutes from our home. I counted my blessings that my wife and I were in the same camp. That sometimes didn't happen. Families were torn apart for no reason. In the end, though, it didn't really matter that we were in the same camp. I never set eyes on her again until we were freed. You see this tattoo on my arm?" Moritz's father paused to show the tattoo. "This number is all I was to them. My life, reduced to a number. You never realize how important your name is until it gets taken away. You start forgetting who you are."

I took a small sip of whiskey, savoring the words Moritz's father was telling me. As much as it pained me to hear this story, I knew that the experience I was having was a unique one. Here I was, a Jew in Germany, only minutes away from a concentration camp with an elder who was now telling me about his own horrific experiences there.

"I escaped once," Mortiz's father continued. "I spent six months planning it. I held on to the underside of a truck for dear life. But it was winter. It was so cold. I've never experienced cold like that since. That was my mistake. Winter. I ended up in the woods but couldn't stay there overnight. The ground was frozen solid. It was snowing. I would have died. I knocked on the doors of my old neighbors, asking for refuge, and was chased away by each one. It wasn't their fault. They were scared for their families. The Nazis would have killed the entire family including their children.

Eventually, I had to return to the camp. It was my only option, other than death. And I couldn't do that to my wife."

Moritz's father paused for a moment, reliving his memories as he spoke them to me. "For trying to escape, I was put in solitary confinement for six weeks. I was lucky they didn't kill me. The guards had instructions to beat me three times per day. Like clockwork. I owe my life to a Polish butcher who used to sell me meat before the war. He was allowed to come in three times a week to deliver milk, bread, and butter for the Germans and while doing so, he would slip over to where the prisoners were. He risked his life for me whenever he did so as he secretly snuck me a pound of butter, which was an extremely rare commodity in those days. I couldn't be more grateful. He was a true hero. And because of his actions, I was able to bribe the guards with the pound of butter to not hurt me as much. Of course, they still did, but the beatings were not as bad. They used to beat us with a truncheon. When I gave them butter, they would hit me less. They'd also hit the wall instead to make it sound like they were still beating me."

Moritz's father paused again and took a breath. "Some days, the Polish man could not come. I was always scared that I wouldn't survive those days. I nearly died more times that I could count. I needed to survive for my family. That's what got me through. Thinking of my wife and our lives together, I prayed so hard every day. I promised God that if I got out of there, I would never break any law. Neither would my family. We would be good people. I would become a man of God, a pious Jew. I later found out that the Polish butcher had a special plant with a plaque dedicated to him in The Garden of The Righteous in Israel, which is devoted to non-Jews who risked their life for us. It doesn't seem like enough though, does it? The man risked his life every day." Pausing, Moritz's father took a deep swallow of his own whiskey. Then, he continued.

"A few years later, we were freed. I fought for my life every single day, for a long time, as did all the other men and women there. You would think that upon being released, everybody would be so excited to return home, that people would have been dancing in the streets and singing. But the people were starved. I don't mean hungry, I mean *starved*. It took years to rebuild our lives. We had to start over. But I'll tell you this, it makes you appreciate what you have. Every day is a blessing to me now."

I could almost see tears in his eyes. Almost. This man brought a whole new meaning to the word "strength." To go through something like what he had experienced and be able to speak about it so candidly was unbelievable to me. As I looked into his eyes, I suddenly realized I needed to get out of that room. I felt feverish and claustrophobic. I thanked both Moritz and his father and told them that I needed to take a walk.

I quickly stumbled out of the room and down the hall. My hands were shaking as I opened the front door and walked out into the street. I turned left, away from the center of the town. That's when I felt the tears coming, stinging the corner of my eyes like needle points. I choked them back, pulled out a cigarette from a pack I had in one of my pockets, and took the biggest drag I could. Sitting on my haunches, on the curb of that unfamiliar town, the story told by Moritz's father weighed heavily on my shoulders. His story rattled around my head over and over. I'm not sure when I started walking again, but I'd walked at least two miles from the house before I realized it and turned to walk back.

I arrived at the family home an hour later. I had decided there was nothing I could say to Moritz's father about the story he'd just told. Nothing I thought of to say seemed right. Can anyone really explain what it is like to walk back into a death camp? He didn't need my sympathy. I decided that I would just respect him. The man deserved to be respected. That felt right to me. I also made up my mind that I would travel to Israel at some point in my life. I had to see the Gardens of the Righteous, where that butcher's plant lived on.

My time in Germany with Moritz's family had a monumental impact on my life. It encouraged me to learn more about my people as I knew very little about Jewish history at the time. I felt as though my life had been incredibly sheltered until now. My eyes had now been opened. I needed more.

Chapter Twelve

A few days later, it was the Fourth of July. Growing up, the holiday had always been a big deal for me, so I was glad when Maurice and Moritz wanted us to celebrate it together. We decided our best bet was to go to the Hofbräuhaus, one of Germany's oldest and well-known beer halls. They served large mugs of perfectly chilled beer, the best I've ever had. Every time we passed the hall when Moritz took us on a tour of Munich, the atmosphere seemed lively, and you were guaranteed to bump into some traveling Americans there, which was an added bonus on this occasion.

We walked into the Hofbräuhaus in the early afternoon that day and didn't leave until three o'clock the next morning. We sang, drank, and took part in Maurice's favorite pastime, chatting up the ladies. As it turned out, the majority of the people in the bar that day were American, and a patriotic party was in full swing. We joined up with a group of around twenty men and women from the States. I spent most of the evening talking to a group of hippie students from Michigan State, all studying the humanities. They spoke of folk music, coffee shops, and festivals. It was my first encounter with hippies; back at Babson, we kept it a little more buttoned up. That is to say, though there were no hippies in Babson, if any did show up, we would have stayed away from them since we didn't really understand them.

By early evening, everyone was pretty drunk. I even noticed Moritz in a corner of the bar kissing one of the hippie chicks. One of the students took out a guitar, and everyone gathered around singing songs by Bob Dylan; Johnny Cash; and Peter, Paul, and Mary. I found myself on top of a long wooden table, spinning around a girl whose face and name I've long since forgotten. I remember looking down and seeing Maurice smiling up at me, that huge, contagious grin. I felt myself grinning back and holding the girl tighter as we pirouetted clumsily.

As the evening wore on, the music mellowed out. Energetic dancing turned into something slower, more mellow. I have no idea whether the girl I ended up with was the girl I started off with, but in my opinion that's the sign of an evening well spent. This time it was, for sure.

A few nights after the Fourth, Moritz took us out to a bar in the University of Munich's student district. Tall and blond, he stood out like a sore thumb walking between Maurice and me with our dark heads of hair. Maybe that's why the girls in the bar took a shine to him straight away. Who knows? Within twenty minutes of walking into the club, I lost both of my friends to beautiful women. Unfortunately for me, I didn't speak much German, and was having a hard time occupying myself. I decided to go and sit at the bar. Perching on top of one of those ridiculously high bar stools, I asked for a "bier." I took the beer from the bartender, giving her the money. Served in a large frosty mug, it was the second-best beer I'd ever had.

I muttered "Dank e." In order to be polite. As I previously stated, I always try to learn at least the basics of the local language wherever I go.

"That's a good German accent you've got there, for an obvious American," the bartender half shouted to me across the racket of the club. I looked up from my "bier" and saw that she was one of the most beautiful women I had ever seen. The image of her face still stands out today and will be ingrained in my mind for the rest of my life. Her skin was honey-colored, her hair almost black. All I can tell you is that when those emerald seafoam eyes stared into mine, I couldn't look away. I don't know why. Maybe it was love at first sight. I can't explain it better than that.

Before long I realized I hadn't answered her!

"Oh," I stammered. "Thank you. So, why are you bartending?" It was the first thing I could think of, and I hoped I didn't come across as rude.

She leaned in closer. "I'm working my way through university."

"Hey, I did the same thing."

"Yeah, well, I've got a sick mother to support." The sadness in her voice seeped out at the mention of her mother. I wanted to be supportive, I really did, but all I could think about was how close her neck was to mine, as a mix of perfume and musk hit me like a brick.

"I'm sorry about your mom," I managed.

She smiled a sad smile and turned away to serve somebody else at the other side of the bar.

I scolded myself for being so awkward. I should have used one of Maurice's stories to get her to stay and talk to me, although she didn't seem like the kind of girl who would fall for that. Drinking the remainder of my beer, I decided I needed to actually talk to the girl I was obsessing over. I caught her laughing with another patron of the bar. Her young fresh face lit up as she was joking with other customers. The smile never reached her eyes. She was so inherently sad. I was drawn to her as I'd never been drawn to anyone before. I felt as though I was being pushed toward her. I drank the last drop of my beer and signaled for her to come over. She walked towards me with a kind of ethereal grace, as if she was floating.

"I'll have another beer please." I said, smiling at her. She walked over and placed it in front of me, holding her hand out for the money. I put the money in her hand as delicately as I could, my fingertips grazing her skin. Her eyes met mine and I swear the sadness went away for a moment.

"Where are you from? I noticed your accent." I said to her, my fingertips retracting from her skin as I reluctantly placed my hands on the table.

"I was born in Russia," she replied, seeming to take note of the look in my eye, the longing to know more about her. "I speak five languages though, including Russian and German, obviously."

I was floored. Who speaks five languages fluently? Not even Maurice, a self-professed man of the world, could speak five!

"You must be incredibly smart," I told her. She seems to like a compliment on her intellect, rather than her appearance, and we chatted for a long time. She kept having to go and serve other people at the bar, however. I remember feeling unjustifiably jealous. Here was this woman I had just met, and every time she spoke to someone else at the bar, my brain started screaming, *NO, COME BACK! PAY ATTENTION TO ME!* I tried my luck at the end of the evening and asked her on a date for the next day. She said yes and told me that she would play hooky from classes and join me for a picnic in the park in the afternoon. That night I fell asleep smiling, dreaming of how tomorrow's date might end up.

When I awoke the next morning, the beers had worn off and realization set in that I had never asked the woman's name! I hoped I could pull off asking her casually. I got dressed, and after spending forty-five minutes preparing myself for the encounter, I headed to the Englischer Garten—a park at the center of Munich. As the name suggests, it is based around English landscaped gardens. The day was scorching hot, and I had already sweated through my shirt when I met my date where she was standing, under an old oak tree. I was thankful for the shade—but even more that I had found her.

Her name was Viktoriya. She laughed when I had to ask and I thanked God for the bullet I had dodged. We decided to take our picnic to the woodland area and find a clearing in which to eat. As luck would have it, we found the perfect spot by a stream, and sat with our toes in the cool iridescent water. The next hour flew by in a flurry of laughter, sandwiches and, yes, again, a few too many beers. We stretched out on the picnic blanket Viktoriya had brought. The beer and the heat had made both of us lightheaded and happy. Looking up at the cloudless sky, with this unbelievably beautiful, smart, and kind woman next to me, I felt like I was in heaven. What more could a young man want? I was just thinking about how fortunate I was when Viktoriya turned to face me, her skirt riding up her tanned leg a little. Her t-shirt slid up to reveal her navel.

Turning to face her, I couldn't stop my hand from reaching out and caressing the smooth skin of her hip. Her breath caught and she pulled herself flush into my body. Leaning in, she kissed me gently at first, then harder and harder. Then, without warning, she stood up and removed every stitch of clothing and stepped into the stream's water. Turning back to look at me with a sultry smile, she held out her hand and gestured for me to follow. Being stark naked in a park, at midday no less, was not something I would have dreamt of doing back home, but I undressed as quickly as I could, nonetheless.

I followed her deep into the water. Her shoulders submerged and the water lapped over her still visible breasts. I swam over to her and picked her up. She wrapped her legs around my waist, kissing me deeply. Then, we moved together, completely in sync. Our bodies were one. I couldn't tell where I ended and she began. We stayed like that for a long time, breathing heavily, our bodies intertwined until as she arched her back and sighed into my neck, the final shivers of sex running through her.

We held each other for a long while, enjoying the ripples of the water on our bodies. We talked of our lives and dreams for the future. She wanted to be a clothing designer, or an artist and move away to live in a big city—

London preferably. My dreams were of a different variety. I needed to learn more about my heritage, my history. I needed to finish this adventure with Maurice. At the moment I couldn't plan beyond that.

As the sun began to set and the sky turned a feverish red, we emerged from the lake and dressed. Our bodies dried quickly from the remaining heat of the day. We said our goodbyes and went in separate directions, exchanging contact information and promising that we would keep in touch. That said, it would be over a year before I heard from Viktoriya again, when she wrote to ask for my help securing a job at Flora's boutique. Her mother had died and she was ready to move to London. She had a bright future ahead of her, and working with Flora in London would be just the beginning of that. As luck would have it, she ended up marrying Flora's then ex-husband. Bizarre as this sounds, no harm was done and everyone involved was happy. I was invited to the wedding, but I respectfully declined.

Chapter Thirteen

Soon after my eventful picnic with Viktoriya, Maurice and I left Germany and headed for the Austrian Alps. I wanted a quiet, calm drive. Maurice, of course, had other plans. It wasn't long before he turned the conversation to the topic of ladies of the night. Maurice said he did not understand why I had yet to partake. The discussion soon became heated, Maurice often gesturing with his hands as he spoke which often meant that he sometimes removed both hands from the steering wheel. When that happened, I had to grab hold of it quickly to keep us on the road.

"Hookers are people too, Garree," he almost shouted. "I don't know why you can't wrap your head around that."

"I know they are people. That doesn't necessarily mean I want to pay to have sex with one of them."

"Garree, that is ridiculous." I could tell, yet again, that Maurice's life had been very different from my own by the fact that he found my argument completely unfathomable.

"Let's talk about something else."

"I know what you want to talk about."

"Oh yeah, what's that?"

"Anything except lovely ladies of the night."

"You got that right."

"Perhaps you'd like to talk about Flora instead?"

"Yes. How is she? She seemed a little sad when we saw her in Paris."

"Flora and her husband are unhappy together. They don't speak much."

Hearing this, some part of me lit up with the unrealistic thought that perhaps I had a chance. I immediately berated myself. Flora was way out of my league. Still, wanting more information, anything to keep him talking about Flora, I asked Maurice why he thought that.

"They hardly live in the same country. Flora, her maid Mina, and little Daria live in London together, but her husband is never there." Daria was Flora's three-year-old little girl, whom Flora loved more than anything in the world. When I had met her briefly in London, she was just as pleasant and well-mannered as her mother, in addition to being the spitting image of her. Between the attention provided by Flora and Mina, the little girl was clearly well cared for and nurtured, despite the fact that, as I now know, she hardly ever saw her father.

"Well, they seem to do okay on their own," I said. "Flora certainly seems like she has things handled."

"Flora owns Mina. Can you believe that? My parents bought her from a poor family, promising her a better life, and gave her to Flora as a wedding present."

Maurice must have seen the look of shock flash across my face. *Did my beloved Flora have a flaw*, I pondered.

"Don't worry, Garree, she's not a slave. I'm joking when I call her that. She is free to come and go as she pleases. Mina is like family. She will never want for anything."

"How often does Flora see her husband?" I asked.

"A couple of times a month, maybe."

The fact that they saw each other that little shocked me as well.

"They have separate houses, separate lives," Maurice continued. "I think Flora would like to live more like I do. But she has the businesses that she built herself, and she has Daria and Mina. Her life is in London. Sometimes I think she feels trapped." Maurice had a really close relationship with his sister and looked saddened at the thought of her not being happy. "Trapped to her life, to her husband, to London." Maurice paused after this, debating whether or not to continue his train of thought. "He's a womanizer, her husband. I always knew it. He doesn't treat Flora right. Who knows what he's off doing when he's not with her? It wouldn't surprise me if he was with other women. I don't know why they're still married. I suspect it's because of my father's feelings about divorce. Flora works so hard, selling dresses to all these famous people for tens of thousands of pounds. She doesn't need him." Maurice banged the steering wheel with his first.

"It shouldn't be like that," I agreed. "Flora should be put on a pedestal. She shouldn't be someone's second choice." I'm pretty sure with my tone that I confirmed to Maurice right then that I was in love with his sister. We both loved her in different ways, but love it was. And as Maurice's closest friend, he loved me too.

We looked at each other for a moment, understanding crossing both our faces. Not long after that, we swapped positions, and Maurice took to the passenger seat. He pressed his head against the window, staring at the scenery as it passed. It wasn't long before he fell asleep, his deep breaths fogging up the glass. This showed to me how comfortable we had become together. I'm not sure if anyone else ever saw this vulnerable side of Maurice, other than Flora, that is. I, therefore, felt like I was sharing a great secret with her.

Arriving in Vienna, we dropped all our things into a hotel room and headed out for lunch. As we walked around the city and looked around, we found a small public house that seemed inviting. As we were settling down at a table, Maurice looked at me, dead seriously and said, "I want us to make a bet."

Intrigued, I asked what the terms of the bet were.

"If the next person who walks through that door is a man, you pay for the hookers tonight. If it's a woman, I pay for them." He said it with an air of conclusion. Maurice had seemingly decided that I would join him in his favorite pastime while we were in Vienna. Saying no at this point would just be putting off the inevitable. Once Maurice had set his mind to it, it was simply just going to happen.

"Fine," I replied, already sensing that I would regret this decision. Maurice wanted me to lose the bet, and so I did. I'm not sure how he rigged the odds, but he needed me to lose. He wanted to prove a point. He also wanted to pay for a hooker to service me. When an elderly gentleman shuffled through the doorway, cane in hand, you could see the glee spread over Maurice's face. He quickly checked himself and returned his face to a neutral look. He had won. He swore that night would be my lucky night.

After lunch, we returned to the room and relaxed there for a while. Maurice left to make a phone call, using the hotel phone, and returned a short while later with a beautiful blonde on his arm. "This is Katarina, your date for the evening," he said to me, practically shoving her into the room and then striding off down the corridor.

Katarina's appearance was in stark contrast with our hotel room. Her red vest and purple velvet skirt seemed almost too bright against the drab beige materials of the room. "Hey handsome," she said by way of introduction, in a strong Austrian accent. I smiled in response. I had no idea what to do in this situation. I could have killed Maurice for, firstly, convincing me to do this, and, secondly, for not telling me *how* to do this. As it turned out, I didn't need to know what to do. Katarina sort of pounced on me, pulling my clothes off and getting down to business.

I did not enjoy my first time with a "professional." I was clumsy and had no idea how I should treat her—what I was allowed to do and what was forbidden. Once we had completed the transaction, if you will, we both got dressed again and perched on the same side of the bed. When I'm uncomfortable, I default to my defense mechanism: talking. During the conversation, I learned that she had gone to college and had $35,000 in the bank. She was trying to save $100,000, so she could move to America, rub shoulders with the elite, and marry the richest old man she could find. She figured it would take her another ten years or so. I laughed at the time, but I wager the house I currently live in that she's in New York City right now, having achieved her dream.

Maurice returned to the room a couple of hours later; Katarina had left me earlier with a business-like handshake. He sat down next to me on the bed. "So, how did it go?" he asked, with his usual cheeky grin.

I told him all about it, including Katarina's big dream to live in America and marry rich and old. He seemed very impressed with Katarina's story, which he decided was actually just a story. Maurice told me that normally hookers say they're only doing it to support a sick relative, which he believed was hardly ever the truth. "You're one in a million, Garree. Trust you to not really enjoy your first time with a professional!"

"Hey, I never claimed to be anything that I'm not."

"That's why you're unique." Maurice's face then took a serious turn. "Garree," he said slowly. "Could you maybe lend me some money?"

I felt like the world had turned on its axis. Here was the prince asking the pauper for change. "Why do you need to borrow money?" I asked. "You're rich."

"I did some bad gambling in London. I couldn't help it. It's in my blood. I'm Persian."

"You never told me you gambled there," I said, quietly. Maurice and I both knew I would lend him the money. It was never a question of that, I was just upset that he felt like he needed to hide it from me. In fact, I had harbored a sneaking suspicion back in London every time I was with Flora, that Maurice might have been gambling. I had hoped I wasn't right. Turns out, I should have probably trusted my gut.

"Garree, I'll pay you back, with interest. Just let me ask my father for some money again. I promise you he'll send it straight away. I just need you to tide me over until it comes."

"You can stick your interest!" I replied, emphatically. Maurice smiled and slapped me on the back.

"Thank you, Garree. Now let me tell you where we are going tonight."

"Hang on a minute, Maurice." I interrupted. "I'll lend you the money, but I don't want you to gamble with it."

"Fine." Maurice said, but his face told me a different story. My stipulation was not fine. So far on our trip, he'd managed to hide quite a lot of his gambling from me. Our conversation that evening told me that there was a lot more going on that I had no idea about.

"How much do you need?" I asked.

"A thousand should tide me over."

"Okay, deal," I said.

"Thank you. Now can I finally tell you about tonight?"

"Shoot."

Maurice had seen a poster for an event that night, which was "black-tie" only. That would be an issue. Neither of us had a tuxedo. The concierge at the hotel we were staying in was very helpful and managed to acquire two tuxedos for us to rent, for a nominal fee. They arrived quickly, in a taxi no less. Leave it to Maurice to borrow money, and then have tuxedos delivered in a taxi. The whole prospect seemed crazy to me as the next time I would wear a tuxedo would be at my wedding. It just confirmed to me that he had no real sense of what money meant.

Dressed to impress, Maurice and I made our way to the event. Vienna was like a fairy tale. All of the buildings throughout the city center were like castles, with spires and gargoyles. The streets were narrow, and on each side of us rose towering fortress-like buildings. We arrived at the address on the poster and found a gated manor house, with huge grass lawns sweeping around the driveway. The gates were open, inviting in the finely dressed guests. Maurice and I gave each other a look that expressed our mutual awe and walked up the driveway. Huge hedges lined the road to the house, giving way to a magnificent fountain which was right in front of the steps that lead up to the front door.

The manor was absolutely packed, full of handsome, and clearly very rich, men with wives glittering in expensive, disco ball like gowns, which could have been designed and made by Flora. Roulette tables were dotted around the room, and all of them had men crowded around them, impatiently waiting for their turns. Their wives stood around the edge of the room in groups, rolling their eyes at how their men were behaving. Maurice went straight over to a group of young wives and immediately immersed himself in conversation, making wild gestures which unsurprisingly made the women burst into flirtatious laughter. Left to my own devices, I stood alone, not daring to approach the ladies and equally not daring to approach the men at the roulette tables. I wished I had thought to bring a book. I was out of my depth here.

The highlight of my evening came when I passed a roulette table and wiped the ashes from someone's cigarette off the green felt, earning myself a fifty-dollar chip from one of the players, which I immediately cashed. Maurice, who was in a good mood after entertaining the young wives for the evening, asked if I would lend him more money so he could have a "little" gamble at the roulette tables. I declined, reminding him of our earlier conversation. I would only lend him more money to extend our trip, and not for it to be gambled away. Maurice, clearly disappointed by my answer, nonetheless plastered his famous smile on his face and said, "Come on then, Garree, let's go home."

Maurice regained his cheerful attitude on the walk home, dancing, laughing, and joking the entire time. He told stories of his conversation with the wives from the party that would make you blush. The women clearly weren't satisfied with their relationships—let's leave it at that. He threw his arm around my shoulders and said, "You're one in a million, Garree," with the biggest grin on his face. Even then, the way he said my name would make me smile. . . .

We chatted about our next adventure, Czechoslovakia, where we would be heading in the next couple of days. Little did we know, we would experience a bit too much excitement there.

Chapter Fourteen

Czechoslovakia was a very desolate place. The barren landscape contained therein made me miserable. Though we occasionally passed towns with small groups of people moving slowly through the streets, Maurice and I didn't know what to think. We drove in silence. The people we passed all looked at the car with dubious expressions, probably because they had never seen a red car like our Mustang before. Sporadically, an individual would shout something at us in a language we couldn't understand, and every time they did so, an uneasy feeling would wash over me.

The Mustang purred along these strange roads, piloted by Maurice's steady hand. As we crossed over a high plain, I saw a fleet of tanks coming over the horizon, and all the color drained from my face. The giant military vehicles crawled along the dusty road toward us like ants. Their slow steady rumble made me feel even worse about the situation. They seemed ominous—harbingers of some unknown doom.

"Garree," Maurice said. "I'm getting a bad feeling."

"Something isn't right," I agreed.

"I had enough of tanks and army men in Paris," Maurice said. "Where are the girls, Garree?"

"No girls here, only lots of gray," I replied.

We decided to spin the car around and head back for the border. When we reached the first checkpoint, we were asked to get out of our vehicle by military officers, guns strapped across their broad chests. They silently escorted us to a holding room.

The holding room resembled the waiting room of a dentist's office. Rows of chairs covered in that sticky sort of plastic that could be easily cleaned of bodily fluids ran parallel to each other, anchored into the floor. I didn't want to think about what substances had been cleaned from the chairs. The officers stood at intervals around the outside of the room, guns in hand, faces unmoving. I was terrified by their stern expressions. They seemed like the type of men for whom taking a life was a task like any other.

Maurice looked even more nervous than I did. His disdain for this holding room was clear—this was not the type of place he cared to spend any time at all. I looked out the window at the rows of tanks lining the border. My thought was that it would make a terrific photo for my family back home. I could tell them I had been imprisoned in a communist country! I pulled out my camera and snapped a photo through the waiting room window. As I looked up from the viewfinder, I saw one of the officers in the corner of the room give me a withering glare. He strode over, took the camera out of my hands, and placed a set of handcuffs around my wrists. It happened in one fluid motion. My shock prevented me from protesting. That said, I don't think protesting would have gotten me far anyway. I sat there, handcuffed next to Maurice. The silence was deafening.

After we had been sitting there in terrified silence for two hours, a convoy of buses showed up at the border, all of which were full of Americans. Amongst them was Shirley Temple Black, the famous child actor who later became the U.S. Ambassador to Czechoslovakia. At this time, Shirley Temple Black was on a committee focused on the Multiple Sclerosis meeting in Prague. However, when the Russians invaded Czechoslovakia, she was asked by the ambassador of Czechoslovakia to escort all of the Americans she could find trapped within the borders of the country. The ambassador made her a Jr. Diplomat so she could have diplomatic immunity.

Ms. Black strode into the waiting room in a navy pantsuit and white button-down blouse, demanding to speak to whomever was in charge there. One of the officials spoke into a walkie-talkie. Moments later, a man appeared, dressed similarly to the other officials, except for the smirk on his face. Arrogance exuded out of his every pore.

"You asked to speak to me?" he asked Ms. Black, peering down at her.

"Yes, I did," she replied indignantly and waltzed out of the room. The haughty officer in charge followed at her heels. She returned a few minutes later with the officer who looked like he'd received a good dressing-down. He muttered some words at the guards around the room, and one came over and undid my handcuffs.

"Follow me," Ms. Black instructed Maurice and me as she led us toward one of the buses. At the bus, she told us that we needed to get into our car and leave that instant. She explained to us that she had recognized the Rhode Island license plate on the Mustang and knew that we would need assistance.

We thanked her passionately several times, and then climbed into our car. We exhaled for what felt like the first time in days as we drove behind the convoy, out of Czechoslovakia, and into Yugoslavia. I was glad Maurice was driving because my hands were shaking like an alcoholic with the DTs.

"Well, that was a close one," I said, wiping my sweaty brow.

"Garree, let me give you some advice I learned in my country," Maurice said. "Cameras and soldiers with guns are usually not a good mix."

"You're not upset with me, are you?" I asked.

"Why would I be upset?" he asked. "I wasn't the one with handcuffs around my wrists."

"Can you believe Shirley Temple saved us?"

"Thank God for American movies, and for the one and only Miss Shirley Temple," Maurice said fervently. We were both altogether impressed at having met her, even under such terrible conditions. We were also very grateful to her, as things could have gotten a whole lot worse if she had not showed up.

In Yugoslavia, the second communist country we visited, everything seemed to be either black, brown, or grey. Houses, clothing, cars, even the people seemed concrete-colored. In our bright red Mustang, we stuck out like a sore thumb, which earned us stares from all the locals. We stopped at a small town to refuel the car and get a bite to eat. After we filled the car, we parked it on the street and walked a short distance to a small café where we took our time eating and drinking. When we returned to the Mustang, we found it surrounded by twenty or so armed Civil Defense soldiers.

"Great," I said. "More soldiers."

"Keep your camera off them," Maurice cautioned unnecessarily.

"Don't worry. I learned my lesson."

The soldiers who buzzed around the car seemed to be searching it thoroughly with their eyes. Maurice puffed out his chest, squared up his shoulders, and walked up to them. It was at this point that we noticed their guns were all propped up against the edge of a nearby building, and that the soldiers were smiling and laughing.

As I walked up, one soldier slapped me on the back and asked in broken English, "Your car?"

"His car," I said, pointing at Maurice. The soldiers were fascinated by the Mustang and their faces shone with glee like little children at Christmas. Their fascination was unreal to me, but I was pretty sure it was the first time they had seen a car like that in real life. Nevertheless, we spent the next hour opening the hood, letting them check out the engine, and sit in the driver's seat. We left the soldiers with huge grins on our faces, feeling like heroes.

We continued driving, hoping to find somewhere we might want to spend the next couple of days. Eventually, we reached a small town typical of communist countries. That is to say, it had a large water fountain at its center and a café not far from the fountain. As we drove through the town while dusk was approaching, we noticed a large group of people entering the only commercial building in town, as if they were going to a meeting. The building itself also contained signs showcasing pictures of booze so we figured it was both a meeting place and a bar. Deciding to join them in the hopes of getting a drink, I pulled the Mustang up in front of it. Entering the building, Maurice and I walked over to the bar and tried to order a drink. The language barrier caused problems for us, and we each eventually ended up with a Coca-Cola bottle. We sat down at a vacant table, and I pulled out a pack of cigarettes, lit one, and began smoking. I did not smoke often, but enjoyed a cigarette every once in a while, and here seemed like as good a place as any.

Maurice nudged me a moment, eyes darting around the room. That said, it took me a short while to understand that he wanted me to look around the room as well. Sure enough, all eyes were on me. Or more specifically, on my cigarette. Not knowing what to do, I went out to the car, got a carton, and brought it back to the hall. I then took a moment to hand out my American cigarettes to people, along with the lighter. The atmosphere in the hall suddenly changed after that, and both Maurice and I became the center of attention. You would have thought we were their long-lost cousins. Men were shaking our hands and hugging us. The ladies were giving us kisses on the cheek. It wasn't long before the locals brought out their handmade instruments that served as their version of guitars, drums, and various kinds of wind instruments. Once everyone was ready, they began to sing songs in their language.

Before we knew it, we had real drinks thrust into our hands, while we were simultaneously pulled up to dance. Some of the women went out and brought food back for us. The locals, however, would not let us spend a dime. I'm sure we were introduced to everyone in the town, but even though no words of conversation were exchanged between us, we felt as though we belonged there. I just kept hearing the word "Americanos."

Never before had I felt so welcome in a town. Maurice left them the biggest tip of our travels thus far, but only after standing on a table and giving a toast. He held his drink in the air and made his usual toast, "Here's to those who wish us well, and all the rest may go to hell!" The residents had no idea what he was saying, but that didn't stop them from cheering along with him.

After all the liquor we were given, God knows how we managed to drive and find a hotel for the evening, but we did. I have no recollection of that journey, however. My next memory is waking up in a soft twin bed with Maurice snoring on the next bed. I rolled over and went back to sleep for a while longer.

Chapter Fifteen

After a few more days enjoying the nightlife, beaches, and clubs in Split, Yugoslavia, a resort city on the ocean, we spent a moment deciding where to go next. Maurice and I needed to figure out whether we were going to head south toward Russia and Iran, or west toward Italy and the South of France. That said, since we had an apartment waiting for us in the South of France, and we were low on funds, the clear choice was easy to spot. Furthermore, another factor which helped make our decision clear was the fact that we might struggle to enter Russia in the first place since Maurice had an Iranian passport. This would have been a problem since the countries were bitter enemies at the time. Even if we did manage to cross the border, we would more than likely be under intense scrutiny. There was also the possibility of meeting the Shah of Iran in the South of France. When you traveled with Maurice, there was always the possibility of meeting royalty.

As such, we made our way west, stopping first in Venice, a very colorful city. Each building seemed to be a different shade of blue, green, yellow, or orange, all of which reflected back to us in the crystalline water that filled the city's canals. The gondolas were the only real method of travel around the city, so Maurice and I relied on them for the entirety of our stay. I always felt thoroughly relaxed each time we sat reclined on the boat, taking in the sites while gently rocking to our destinations.

My favorite thing about Venice was the people themselves. They were so friendly and funny, their olive-skinned faces always smiling. However, those smiling faces and their sense of humor lured us into a false sense of security. After a few days, we figured out that the gondola workers had been scamming us, taking us on slightly longer routes and gouging up the price. We figured this out one day when it took us twenty minutes to go for a five-minute ride.

When Maurice questioned the gondola driver about this, he shrugged his shoulders, pretending not to understand us. Not getting the explanation he wanted, Maurice became frustrated and ended up throwing his shoes at the smirking Italian. The sight of Maurice hopping around, red-faced, trying to free his shoes from his own feet, would, under any other circumstance, have been hilarious to me. Though it probably was extremely humorous to passers-by, it definitely was to the Italian, who gained a lovely pair of new loafers out of the debacle.

Shoeless and sulking, Maurice eventually led me into what was our destination for the evening, a small building painted with muted colors. Maurice explained that due to his lack of appropriate footwear, this was the only place that would let us dine there. It was a dive in every sense of the word. Old, rough-hewn wooden tables were spaced unevenly around the room, while mismatched chairs were placed around them in random odd numbers. The air, furthermore, was thick with tobacco smoke, exhaled from the sour mouths of elderly men positioned at the dirty tables. It was by far the worst place I had ever eaten, but it was cheap and that suited our new monetary restrictions. It took three showers that evening to wash the smell from my body and hair. My clothes, however, never smelled the same again.

The next night, after Maurice had bought himself a new pair of shoes, we dined at The Casino of Venice, a classier establishment. I didn't want to go gambling again, but there was no stopping Maurice when he wanted something badly enough. He knew how to play people and get what he wanted. That was the Persian in him, he'd always say.

We made our way to the casino via gondola again, but this time, we made sure we were taken by the most direct route. When we arrived, we climbed out of the gondola as gracefully as we could in our suits and stepped onto the small wooden docking area outside the casino. The building looked magnificent in the dusky twilight as it towered above the canals, monumental in stature. Each story of the building was lined with windows surrounded in iron. One simply couldn't help but stop and stare.

Walking into the building, I felt like I was stepping into a different world. Whereas the outside was archaic, the inside was modern and filled with colorful, though somewhat flashy furniture that screamed luxury and comfort. The reception area, furthermore, was surrounded by immense sweeping staircases leading to the various floors. We followed easy to understand Italian signs and arrows that led up the stairs and to the left toward the restaurant, treading easily on the luxurious red patterned carpeting in our dress shoes.

Arriving at the restaurant, we were treated like royalty and led to a two-seater table draped with fine white linen tablecloths and an imposing glass candelabra between us. It may have been due to Maurice's good looks and persuasive charm, or maybe it was because I was an American dressed in a white sport jacket with a black see-through shirt. Whatever the reason, they waited on us hand and foot. The food, by the way, was absolutely delicious. Three courses, and too many glasses of champagne to count later, we headed off into the casino itself.

Walking across the mezzanine from the restaurant to the casino, we decided to stop for a minute and look over the wooden railing. We were on the second floor, and from where we stood, you could see directly into the reception area. I expected the same atmosphere we had seen in the other casinos we had visited on our trip thus far, but what I saw was the exact opposite. That is to say, while the atmosphere in the casino room was indeed livelier than the entrance to the building, it was still subdued for a casino. Men and women were happily chatting with each other as they walked slowly to their destinations, taking their time and enjoying the ambiance. This made me feel more at home as the casino was classier than the ones we had recently been to. It wasn't as noisy as most, and drinking wasn't allowed in the gambling area. As such, I knew then that it wasn't necessarily going to be a crazy night of gambling and losing all of our money.

I made a deal with Maurice to steer clear of the roulette tables. I didn't like the odds, so the game of choice tonight was baccarat. In baccarat, whoever gets closest to nine with two cards wins.

"We'll go halves tonight," Maurice said. "We put in equal money, and whatever we win we split."

"Deal."

Maurice quickly found a free table and perched himself on the high stool. I stood off to the side to let Maurice do his thing. Though we could gamble using liras (Italian currency), our winnings could get exchanged for dollars. A very useful procedure, I felt. Between us, we had decided that our limit was $300. If we lost $600, we would quit. If we won $1,000, we would quit. However, with Maurice, the rules didn't apply as soon as he started playing. He was quickly up $2,000. Did he stop then? No, of course not. I had started begging him to quit since he hit $1,000, but my pleas went unheeded. Fed up with him not listening to me, I decided to take a walk. I wandered around the entire casino which took about an hour. When I returned, Maurice was up $3,500. My nerves were in tatters. Again, I begged him to stop. He waved me away with a signature "Don't worry." He didn't even turn to look at me.

"Come on, Maurice," I said. "If you walk away now, that's enough to keep us flush for the entire rest of the trip."

"Just let me do this, Garree."

"Maurice, walk away!"

I knew I had no chance of getting through to him, so I took another, even longer walk. This time, I decided to ask what time the casino would be closing, as it was already very late in the evening. A member of the staff told me that the casino didn't close, but that we would have trouble catching a gondola home after two in the morning. I decided to find Maurice to tell him this news. He must have realized that my patience and his luck was wearing thin as he handed me $15,000 in chips, instructing me to swap it for paper cash. This left him with some small change to play a little bit of roulette while I went to exchange the chips.

I didn't want to risk carrying those chips around for longer than necessary, so I ran like hell to cash them in. At an exchange rate of 650:1, I ended up being given two large bags of money.

Maurice came over immediately after and met me outside of the exchange booth. Clutching the bags to my chest for dear life, I headed outside to the nearest canal. Maurice hailed a gondola and I stepped in with help from the gondolier. The thought of dropping the money into the water made me sick to my stomach. On the ride back, we basked in the fact that we had made enough money to last us for the rest of the trip, and then some. Man did I feel lucky. My money woes were over! I didn't have the luxuries that Maurice did. I had no Daddy Big Bucks, sister, or business associate to call on, let alone his magic abilities to talk his way into a hotel suite. So much for our agreement! Okay, maybe Maurice sometimes took advantage of people and had conned me into believing we could actually "make our money stretch," but still, I felt lucky.

When we arrived at the hotel, I split the money into two equal piles of

$7,500 and gave Maurice one of them. We then each stored the money in our own bureaus. It took me forever to fall asleep that night due to all of the excitement we had experienced. That said, I woke up the next morning with a weird feeling, sensing that something was out of place. Blinking against the harsh light streaming through the open window, I rolled over. The bed where Maurice should have been was empty. I quickly pulled on my clothes from the night before and checked that my half of the cash was still in my bureau. With a sigh of relief, I saw that it was. A quick check of Maurice's bureau showed me, however, that he'd taken his with him. I immediately knew where he was.

On my way out, I deposited my money into the hotel safe and quickly found a gondola to take me to the casino. I was so angry at Maurice for sneaking around and lying to me that my fists were clenched in frustration for the entire gondola ride there. I marched with purpose into the Casino of Venice and straight over to the roulette tables. I spotted him swiftly, his shoulders hunched in a way I had not seen before. His eyes were bloodshot. His face was contorted into a grimace of concentration, silently pleading for the game to go his way. Maurice didn't notice me until I tapped him on the shoulder, making him jump.

Looking at the expression on my face he said, "Look, Garree. It's fine. I've got the thousand dollars I owe you. Now leave me alone." He thrust a $1,000 chip into my hand in a manner that concerned me. This wasn't the Maurice I knew. The Maurice I knew could stop gambling if he needed to. This was more than being a "typical Persian," and I could see clear as day in that moment that he had a real problem.

"Leave if you want. You can take the car," Maurice said a moment later. "If you want me to come with you, you need to let me win. I'm going to beat the casino, Garree." Of course, I could not leave him; we had come this far together. Even if Maurice lost everything, the $7,500 back at the hotel plus the $1,000 chip he had just given me would see us through the rest of our trip. And why was I worrying about money anyway, I chided myself. After all, right or wrong, and whether I liked it or not, it seemed that one phone call to daddy from Maurice would bring a torrent of gold in on a flying carpet.

I decided to leave him be. In Maurice's head, he clearly needed to do this. I cashed in my chip and went for the longest walk of my life around Venice. I say "walk," but it was a mixture of gondolas and walking. This was Venice after all.

By the time I returned to Maurice, it was 3 p.m., and Maurice was on his final $100 chip. He was a defeated man, not caring anymore whether he lost or won. He placed the chip on red, his eyes meeting mine. He lost a moment later. An understanding passed between us then, and we made our way back to the hotel in silence. We were brothers, and we both knew it. I had seen a side of Maurice that no one had ever seen—the naïve, uncertain side. The side with a problem. Neither of us mentioned this day again. We slowly packed our bags, loaded up the Mustang, and set out for Milan.

The atmosphere on the drive to Milan was subdued. That said, he wanted to talk, to get things off his chest. "Garree," he said, "most Iranians are paid two cents an hour and the majority of people there can't even afford toilet facilities in their homes. That's a few more reasons why I can't go back there. To live, I mean," he told me.

"Where will you live after this trip?" I asked.

"Boston for a while, but London is where I will settle down. I absolutely love it there."

"What will you do there? Work for Flora?"

"Never!" Maurice said with a little laugh. "I don't know what I'll do. I'm not worried though. I always make something happen." Suddenly, the confident Maurice was back, and I have to say, I had missed him.

Over the course of the long car ride, the conversation progressed from his country to his father. I had previously heard bits about Maurice's father, but it was not a topic of conversation Maurice brought up often. That said, I was thrilled when Maurice decided to tell me how his father had made his fortune, as that was one topic I had been secretly dying to know.

"My grandparents saved enough money for my father to go to college in Paris, but not enough for him to be accepted by my mother's parents," he told me. "My father's parents were by no means poor, compared to the majority of people in Iran, but their wealth was nothing compared to my mother's parents." He paused, and then continued.

"My father had to work part-time in a department store throughout his studies in order to stay afloat. He worked in the gift wrapping department, wrapping other people's purchases. Funnily enough, my father's brother Habib was working alongside him at this point. My uncle Habib was much more outgoing than my father, by the way. I consider him the soul of the family. Anyway, one evening, they were wrapping up plastic combs that a customer had bought when my dad had an idea. Somehow, they managed to get credit and bought a boatload of those combs really cheap and shipped them to Iran. My father quit college right after selling the first boatload of combs to sell other products, which one of his brothers had bought in Paris. Then, after obtaining enough money, they invested in more combs. He then recruited his other brothers and after explaining his idea to them, they all joined. If you didn't know, combs were very popular in Iran at the time, but they were hard to attain there. After easily selling those combs, they invested in light bulbs, and sold those even more quickly."

Maurice smirked with pride as he continued. "Before you knew it, they had enough money to build a factory in Tehran, the capital of Iran—a plastics factory, the first of its kind in the country. It could produce practically anything, as long as it was made from plastic. Their profits were astronomical. My father and uncles then kept investing their money in other ventures, such as land and mines. At some point, my father's success was noted by my mother's parents, and they accepted him to be her husband."

Maurice took a breath before continuing. "Once he became successful, everything my father touched turned to gold, figuratively speaking. Oil was discovered on one of his plots of land—a plot of land he bought for a pittance. Though he avoided fame, he went after fortune. He wanted the best for his family after all. These days, he does business all over the world, in over twenty countries. My uncle John handles the investments in the States. A third of all the profits made in Iran go straight into U.S. investments. It's a good system."

Maurice paused to mull over his next few words and then continued. "I admire my father. He's unbelievable. But I don't want to be him. I could never compare to him anyway. I need to forge my own way. If Flora can do it, so can I. I know you doubt me, Garree, but I can put the work in when I need to. I can make something out of myself, you know. Most of all, I want to be an honest man in the business world. I don't want to invest in twenty countries, all under different names. That might work for my dad, but that's not the way I want to be. I want to do things my way. The problem is that I can't get away from his reputation, his influence. It's suffocating."

We sat in silence for a while after this. The weight of his words was a physical presence in the car, pushing us down into the hot material of the seats.

When we finally got to Milan, Maurice's attitude changed. The happy-go-lucky Maurice was back. All the seriousness brought on by our stay in Venice and the journey to Milan was forgotten. That said, we stayed in the area just long enough for Maurice to "spend the night" with a couple of women and for us to see Leonardo da Vinci's Last Supper painting the very next day. There were sandbags from the floor to the bottom of the painting so I surmised that the painting was sandbagged during World War II, in the hope that it would not be destroyed. That story, along with the painting itself made me realize once again that things can change in an instant, and that life is fleeting.

Chapter Sixteen

Our next stop was Switzerland. Though I thought the Austrian Alps were unbeatable, the Swiss Alps were truly magical and driving over them is definitely an experience I will never forget. Every direction I looked, the scenery was awash with greens and blues. The colors were so intense that it looked as though everything had been painted in the most expensive oil paints money could buy. It felt like the clouds were right above my head and easily reachable if I wanted to touch them.

After coming down from the mountains, we arrived in Geneva, exhausted and disheveled from the long drive. The first thing Maurice did was telegram his father. He had been building up the courage to do this, as Maurice's father had some quite strict rules when it came to gambling. Maurice could gamble as much as he wanted, provided he did not lose. I saw in that a lack of intelligent parental guidance and a huge problem for anyone who could possibly believe that you can gamble and never lose.

After picking up our mail from the nearby Ritz-Carlton hotel, we returned to the hotel we were staying in. That evening, we sat on the balcony of the hotel and drank whiskey out of tumblers. Maurice was quieter than usual which I figured was due to his anticipation over his father's response to the telegram he had sent asking for money. I don't believe he was worried that the money wouldn't come; I believe he was worried that his father would be disappointed in him for gambling, and that it had the potential to take over his life.

The next morning, I awoke to a loud knocking at the hotel room door. Staggering there, half asleep, I managed to open the door. At the other side of the threshold was a man in a very expensive suit. "Is Maurice there?" he demanded to know.

"Maurice, someone's here for you," I shouted through to the bedroom, guiding the man through to the living area. I had no qualms about letting the man in. Due to how sharply he was dressed and his demeanor, I could tell he was important. I suspected he was a member of hotel security or the police. I couldn't have been more wrong.

Maurice stepped into the living area, blinking against the sunlight that was pouring in through the half-open patio door. "I'm Maurice," he said, his tone calm and measured. He clearly knew something I didn't.

"Identification please," the suited man responded.

Maurice dug through his bag and produced his passport. The early morning visitor took the passport and checked the picture to confirm Maurice's identity. He then nodded and handed Maurice his passport, as well as an envelope containing 100 dollar bills, before turning on his heels and walking back out the door. When I asked what my morning wake-up call was about, Maurice told me it was money from his father.

"How did you do that?" I asked. "It's Sunday and there are no banks open in Switzerland."

"Did I not mention he owns the Swiss-Israeli National Bank?" he asked with his signature smile.

Even though it was a weekend and no wiring offices were open in Europe,

Maurice's father had found a way to get the money to him. Maurice then continued, "My father woke up the bank manager in the middle of the night and instructed him to get the money to me via courier."

Maurice slapped me on the back, put his arm around my shoulder, and said, "You're one in a million, Garree. What did you *think* was happening? That I was going to be arrested?"

"After your performance in Venice, I thought that anything was possible."

"Venice is forgotten. The past. Now we look to the future. Go back to bed. We have a busy night ahead of us." Following Maurice's orders, I sank back into my twin bed and was asleep in seconds.

Though we remained in Geneva during the day, every night we would cross the border back into France so as to make our way to a world-famous resort and spa town called Évian-les-Bains (the resort and spa town is technically called Évian-les-Bains, but Maurice and most Americans typically call it Évian) located thirty minutes away. Maurice continued to gamble, but I kept him in check, and together, we made sure he didn't burn through his father's money. One evening though, when we had returned to our hotel room, the strangest thing happened. We had fallen asleep on the sofas situated near the balcony after drinking our fair share of scotch, but at some point during the night, a noise woke me up. In my alcohol-addled state, I wasn't sure what was happening, but I did recognize that the noise came from the balcony doors opening. I rolled over, knocking my half-empty glass of scotch to the floor. The loud crash it made on the tiles was enough to pull me out of my drunken haze. I looked up and saw Maurice standing on the balcony, his white shirt sticking to his body like it was soaking wet.

What was he doing on the balcony in the early hours of the morning, I wondered. Then, I noticed something that made my blood run cold. He wasn't standing on the balcony; he was standing at the other side of the wrought iron railing, clinging to the smooth metal.

"Maurice, what are you doing?" I called out in the most normal voice I could muster. I didn't want to startle him. When he didn't reply, I began to move slowly closer to him.

"Maurice?" I tried again. The veins in my head felt like they were going to explode. Surely, he wasn't thinking of jumping! The Maurice I knew would never do such a thing. Stepping closer to him, I started to panic as he wasn't reacting to my calls. He had to have heard me as he was only a few meters away. That's when I realized that he wasn't aware of what was happening. He was sleepwalking.

"Oh, dear God! Please let him be safe," I repeated over and over in my mind for what felt like an eternity. I had heard the rumors about sleepwalkers: that you weren't supposed to ever wake them up. Heeding this advice, I made my way over to him as quietly as I could on the tiled floor. I hesitated before grabbing his shoulder, and then turned him around to face me. Thank God he was pliable. With my gentle coaxing, he returned first one leg, then the other, back onto the safety of the balcony, while never once opening his eyes.

I nearly collapsed with relief as I guided Maurice to the sofa. I didn't think it was a good idea for me to take him to his bed and have him wake up in a different place than where he fell asleep. As I turned him around to sit him on the sofa, Maurice's eyes opened. He looked panic stricken when he looked at me.

"Garree," his voice wavered. "What are you doing to me?" I could tell by way he said these words that he was trying to make a joke, but his poker face faltered.

"You were sleepwalking, Maurice. I was guiding you back to the sofa."

"Where did you find me? I'm freezing!" He slid his mask back up, his façade never failing for long.

"You were on the balcony." I didn't want to tell him the specific details of where he actually was on the balcony.

"I dreamed I was going to jump, Garree!" The humor in his voice almost masked his panic. Almost.

"Thank God you didn't really do it then, Maurice." I tried to lighten the tone of my voice, but I was never one to be able to hide my emotions well.

"Well, thanks, Garree," he said and lay back down on the sofa.

After locking the patio doors, I lay back down on the other sofa, too afraid to fall asleep. What had happened to Maurice to make him dream that he was jumping? I tried hard to clear my mind of what could have happened. When I finally heard Maurice's breathing even out, I went and refilled my glass of scotch and sat back on the sofa. I stared at the balcony doors for a minute, thinking of how differently this night could have gone. The thing that scared me the most, other than losing my best friend, was the phone call I would have had to make to Maurice's father, explaining what had happened. That thought alone almost killed me.

I never mentioned the episode again, but I knew it was etched into his mind as deeply as it was into mine. Nevertheless, we continued on with our adventure, each making a silent vow that we would never speak of it to each other. We drove to Évian where we had some beautiful meals, and Maurice did some gambling. A few days later, we headed off to Nice as though nothing had happened.

In Nice, we were greeted by sunshine. The weather was beautifully warm, the hazy heat reflecting off the surfaces of the terracotta houses. Maurice concentrated on driving slowly along the coast, as I took in the sights: the sapphire sea, white beaches, and bikini-clad women. Eventually, we turned up a windy road into the hills. After about ten minutes of precarious driving on tiny roads, what could only be described as a mansion emerged from behind a hill.

"This is home for the next ten days," Maurice told me proudly. "My dad bought the apartment building as an investment years ago."

I remember thinking to myself at the time, *So it's not a mansion, it's lots of smaller mansions.*

"There are four penthouse apartments," Maurice explained. "One of them belongs to me, but I typically use Flora's when I'm in Nice."

"Any other residences scattered throughout Europe I should be aware of?" I asked.

"Garree, you don't know the half of it."

I was sure that I didn't.

We parked in an underground garage before Maurice took the lead and guided me up four flights of stairs to the top floor. He then proceeded to open the door to the room we would be using. Well, I say "room," but it was actually eight rooms. The other three penthouse apartments were for Maurice, Sharit, and his parents. Maurice showed me to my private bedroom, complete with a king size bed and en suite bathroom. I knew right then that the next ten days were going to be magnificent. I not only had access to the ridiculous apartment, but we also had a balcony, a full kitchen, a car, and our very own tour guide—Maurice himself. To add to all this, the sound of running water from the Évian water factory directly across the street created a magnificent ambience.

The next morning, I took Maurice out for breakfast. I wanted to do something nice for him after the huge amount of generosity he was showing me. After telling him what I had planned, Maurice chose a café next to the train station. I had no idea why until I saw a group of young American girls emerge from a train carriage, laden with huge rucksacks on their backs. Maurice's eyes lit up when he saw them.

Leaning in closer to me, he whispered, "This is why we're here, Garree. The American tourists travel through the night on trains between Nice and Rome because it's cheaper than getting a hotel room for the night." As soon as he finished saying that, he walked right over to the ladies and began chatting away. I watched Maurice work his magic from my comfy seat at the café. Maurice not only had the charm to bag these women, he was also able to offer free room and board—a prospect that the traveling women found most appealing. I will leave what transpired next to your imagination, but I will tell you this one thing. If we had a turnstile that collected coins in our respective bedrooms, I would have earned a lot more money than Maurice. He wasn't fond of American girls. He believed American girls loved you for what you earned, and European girls loved you for who you were. He wasn't about to tell these girls what he earned.

I'm pretty sure Maurice's favorite part of being in Nice was being able to show off his knowledge of the area to me, and as such, we spent some leisurely days exploring the sights and the beaches. Maurice took me to St. Tropez, where Brigitte Bardot lived, and to Juan-les-Pins, where the mayor was only seventeen years old, and parties happened every night between 6 p.m. and 6 a.m. We spent the evenings in high-end places such as Monte Carlo and Cannes, dining and clubbing. Just like always, anytime we went clubbing, Maurice became surrounded by adoring groups of people as he chatted them up and gambled. I, myself, was satisfied by the American women who kept me company back at the apartment. But I also enjoyed the ambiance of the clubs, letting loose and having a good time in my own way.

That said, one thing that happened on the beach in Nice shocked me down to my toes. To this day, I still can't believe what Maurice did. We were sitting there on the sand directly across from the Negresco Hotel, and suddenly, over a handheld microphone, I heard "Telephone call for Moise Elghanayan." I thought that someone had died and turned to my friend since Moise was his given name (he used the name Maurice mostly in the U.S.). "Maurice, is everything okay?" I asked. "Is someone sick? What's the problem?"

"Don't worry, Garree," he said with his trademark big grin. He then said to me, "I will be paying the page boy twenty-five dollars an hour to hold a handheld microphone and yell my name while walking up and down the mile-long beach."

"Why would you do that?" I asked as I looked at the page boy who held the handheld microphone. I did remember seeing a booth on the beach that would charge people for making announcements.

"It's so that when people are looking for me, they will know where to find me," he said in response. I didn't need to ask whether it was people of the male or female persuasion he was hoping would find him since I already knew the answer. Occasionally, if he had been especially nice to me during the next three days we spent in this manner, I would pay the page boy to send out a page for Maurice. It was a simple, yet cost-effective way to thank him for the trip.

Among the lessons I was learning during our stay in Nice, there was one that would stay with me for the rest of my life. One day, we went to a casino—obviously Maurice's idea—where you could use and collect money of any variety. It was incredibly sophisticated, exactly what you would expect from a casino in Nice. No drinking was allowed in the gambling area of the casino, its dress code was strictly enforced (sport jackets were required for men, and dresses for women), and the décor had an air of luxury about it. Before hitting the tables, we went to the bar to get ourselves a beer. We then spent a few moments drinking while perched on bar stools, looking around. While we did so, Maurice noticed me intently watching a well-dressed young man, roughly our age, who was with an incredible looking blonde woman. Around his neck, he wore several thick, expensive looking gold chains. I also saw a gold Rolex peeking out from under his suit-jacket sleeve. Maurice and I continued to watch this man as he sat at one of the tables gambling $1,000 a hand.

Maurice pointed out the sweat dripping from his forehead. He then leaned close to me and whispered, "Don't watch him anymore; he's pretending to be something he's not."

"What do you mean?"

"It's all an act. Can't you see the panic in his eyes, his sweat dripping on to the table? See how tense his shoulders are. He can't afford to be here. It's a façade."

"You're right," I said, noticing it all now.

"This is who you should be watching instead of him," Maurice said, gesturing across the room to an elderly man in casual clothes. "Watch him and you'll learn that things are not always as they seem."

Watching the old man intently, I soon realized what Maurice was talking about. The old man was playing Banco, a game where you play against the banker, not the others at the table. You pull one card at a time, aiming to get as close to nine as possible. There was a pretty slim chance for the old man to win, but that didn't seem to deter him—just as winning also didn't seem to overly affect him.

Maurice must have been watching me the entire time, because he interrupted my train of thought by saying, "You've got it, haven't you, Garree?"

Nodding, unable to take my eyes from the old man, I explained, "He isn't playing with chips and hasn't placed a card. He called Banco at the last minute. He won $100,000 and then walked away like it was nothing. That's the man with money, not the other guy. Right? A man with real money doesn't feel the need to show it off."

"Exactly," said Maurice proudly. "Did you notice that the well-dressed man stormed away from the table when he lost his money? He clearly didn't have enough to be gambling a thousand dollars at a time. Did you also notice the pit boss pocket the thousand-dollar chip he gave him, and note the old man's winnings on his tab?" I nodded again. Maurice continued, "The pit boss gave it to the head cashier, who will take those winnings to the bank for the guest."

Maurice was right; I had not even realized at the time that the old man hadn't even waited to check that the banker had added the winnings to his tab.

This lesson stayed with me—to never judge a book by its cover, or a man by his clothes. Appearances mean nothing. It's what's inside that counts. Often, your first impressions of somebody can be vastly mistaken. Maurice taught me to look deeper, beyond the smokescreens and glitter. To see people for who they really are.

Chapter Seventeen

We drove the Mustang to La Siesta the next evening. A row of Lamborghinis, Rolls-Royces, and Ferraris waited outside the club for their owners. La Siesta was highly exclusive and incredibly expensive—a den of pleasure where the rich and famous of the South of France spent their time and money.

We piloted past the club's ostentatious marquee, and Maurice parked the Mustang in the spot near the beach he usually parked in during his previous visits. He parked here not to avoid paying the parking attendants, or because he was ashamed of the Mustang—he just wanted to show me a rather large billboard that was situated in front of the beach. It was an advertisement for La Siesta, captioned: "Only People of Class, Character, and Elegance May Enter Here."

"Does that include us?" I asked, only half-joking, as we parked.

By way of answer, Maurice turned on his heels and walked so fast that I had to rush to keep up. As in London, Maurice ignored the line of people waiting and waltzed straight to a velvet rope that served as the club's entrance. I tagged along, still seriously doubting I was a person of class, character, and elegance. Not surprisingly, because I was with Maurice, the bouncers parted, and I was allowed to access this strange kingdom.

Inside, the first thing I noticed was the people. Some were dressed in finery, others in casual clothes that still looked exorbitantly expensive. Moreover, some sported bright colors and patterns, while others were clad in monotone suits. Everybody, and I mean *everybody*, seemed to really be getting along and because of this, I got the sense that everyone knew each other. Even though I was a stranger, the atmosphere was so friendly that I immediately felt comfortable.

As Maurice led me to the bar, I looked around and saw that the place was a series of giant rooms under thatched roofs. There was no electricity. Instead, the columns holding the roofs up were lined with gigantic torch lights and large cages filled with bats, hanging from branches situated within the cages. As I learned later, these were colorful, exotic, and expensive bats from all over the world. Why bats? As Philippe, the manager, later explained, "The owners felt that these bats are like our patrons. They sleep all day and play all night."

The only other light illuminating the establishment came from the moon bouncing off of what had to be the biggest indoor swimming pool I had ever seen in my life. Moreover, because there was a full moon, the club was bathed in a twinkling, beautiful haze. What had I wandered into? As I continued to look around in amazement, I couldn't help but notice by the European clothes most people were wearing that I was one of very few Americans there. It seemed like I was not the clientele La Siesta was trying to attract.

Of course, Maurice knew the manager, and said so to the first employees we met. The manager's name was Philippe, and Maurice's father had been sending him a $1,000 check every Christmas. Philippe, in turn, used the money to buy his children and wife gifts on Christmas. I should have expected that Maurice had connections at this club. Although there was a large line of people in fancy clothes waiting for tables, we were ushered right past them and to Phillipe himself. He smiled, exchanged pleasantries with us, and then seated us at a large and beautifully set table overlooking the pool, which was cloaked in moonlight. The whole ambiance made it seem like I was in a dream. We settled in for an amazing meal: wine and a pair of steaks for Maurice and myself. I believe it was Philippe who ordered the food on our behalf, for we certainly didn't order anything.

After I had eaten my fill, I told Maurice I wanted to take a walk around the club and then shortly thereafter left him to continue enjoying his dinner. Inside La Siesta, there were several unique rooms (one seemed to be extra fancy, which made me think it was for weddings), bars, and a massive swimming pool. In one room, every table showcased a different theme. For instance, the chairs at one table were race car themed, while they looked like airplane seats at another table. One table even had swings instead of chairs! As I walked around, I saw people gyrating wildly to music on the concrete lily pads that formed stepping stones across the pool. I also saw two incredibly large speakers cordoned off by velvet ropes so as to prevent patrons from getting closer than fifteen feet of them and having their eardrums blown off. Either way, I was a little drunk on wine and without a care in the world, or a thought in my head, and as such, decided to join the party. Soon enough, I found myself dancing on one of the pads on top of La Siesta's large swimming pool while staring at beautiful women in mind blowing outfits, including skin tight blouses and hot pants. *It doesn't get any better than this*, I thought to myself.

After a particularly sensual song ended, I hopped off the pad and walked around in a daze, my mouth hanging halfway open. Eventually, I found myself on a wide terrace that opened up onto the beach. I could see massive yachts moored to the water and tenders transporting guests back and forth. This suggested that the area was being used by people of another level of wealth entirely. The soft lights coming from the terrace bounced off the hulls of the boats, cloaking the beach in an atmospheric glow. It was the most romantic setting I had ever seen.

Other people must have agreed because there were a few couples actually engaged in love making right there on the beach, their silhouettes moving as rhythmically as the tide. I remember thinking that I would love to someday bring someone I loved here and try that.

Walking back to meet Maurice, I detoured around the indoor pool and saw girls dancing on podiums to thumping French house music provided by a DJ. Other dancers surrounded the pool, spilling into doorways and seating areas, jumping and swaying in time to the music beneath the club's thatched roofs.

I found Maurice by the bar, cool as a cucumber. My head was reeling from everything I had seen, and I felt like I needed to leave and come back to La Siesta when I was better prepared.

"Maurice. I think my mind is about to explode from all that I have seen."

"No problem, Garree," Maurice said. "It's a lot to take in for one night."

"Let's come back tomorrow," I replied.

On the way to the car, Maurice said, "Garree, did you know that the last person to leave La Siesta is always given a bottle of champagne on the house? Though that doesn't usually happen until the sun rises." Maurice smiled for a moment before he turned to me again. "Let's go to Club Vallone! The manager of La Siesta usually hangs out there late at night."

"Maurice. Can we do that another night? Please? I need sleep." Tomorrow would be a new day. For the time being I was overwhelmed and really needed to go to bed.

Chapter Eighteen

The next morning, I began to understand why Maurice had told me to leave the South of France until the end of our trip—nothing could possibly compare to it. We drove to Cannes to see what the rich and famous were up to and soon neared the idyllic stretch of beach, and the iconic boardwalk where you could bump into famous people all day long. Unlike Nice, the beach at Cannes contained smooth clean white sand, and no rocks. The area was also chock full of colorful houses and beautiful people like Sophia Loren, Gina Lollobrigida, and even Brigitte Bardot. My heart began to race. I had no idea what was in store, but I knew it was going to be memorable.

"The only problem with Cannes," Maurice said, as we neared the center of the town, "is that it was built many years before it became popular. People come at 6 a.m. and take up all the spots, so there is nowhere to park."

"Where the heck *are* we going to park then?" I asked.

Maurice responded with his trademark grin, then pulled up in front of the Ritz-Carlton.

As it turned out, he was old friends with the head attendant at the garage. Andrew, a young redhead, always gave Maurice preferential treatment over the famous that flocked to this stretch of sand. I listened as they filled each other in on what had happened to each other in the past year or so since the last time they last met. Andrew joked that he had watched Maurice grow from an inexperienced womanizer to a sophisticated wooer of women.

After we parked, Maurice showed me the movie theatre where they held the Cannes Film Festival. I personally found it to be a bit gaudy. We ate at a restaurant next door, feeling like movie stars. To my surprise, I managed to pay the bill before Maurice. I remember that because it was a rather hefty bill. I was happy to pay it though, as I always was with my generous friend.

Maurice wanted to catch up with Andrew for a bit after lunch, so I headed down to the beach. The ocean that day was a shade of blue I have not seen since. It was also so clear you could see the ocean floor. Schools of brightly-colored fish glided by serenely, much like the fancy patrons of La Siesta. I felt as though I had arrived in a corner of the universe designed just for me, for my happiness.

Towards the evening, Maurice and I headed to St. Tropez for supper. It was part of the French Riviera ten or so miles from Cannes. Nothing really exciting happened there, which helped give my mind some rest. On the drive home, Maurice noticed an advertisement for the Rolex Yacht Cup races.

"Garree, this is something we need to do," he enthused.

"The races are tomorrow," I said. "How are you going to get a boat that quickly?"

"Oh, I know a guy. Don't worry Garree," he said, smiling, assured as ever.

Maurice did indeed "know a guy." Maurice used a pay phone to reach him and after exchanging pleasantries and explaining that he and his guest wanted to see the Rolex Yacht Cup races, they agreed to meet. We met him soon after at an out of the way port down a dirt road. The captain, or Captain John as he liked to be called, was about fifty-five years old and looked like an old sea dog with his salty hair and captain's hat. He welcomed us aboard his boat the "True Love," and explained that he had competed in the Rolex Yacht Cup races a year or so before. He had even come in at third place during one of them.

As we entered the boat, we found two young ladies who were nurses from South Africa and had just returned from a two-year job in Saudi Arabia. When you're renting a boat, women seem to just appear.

Anyway, that afternoon, the captain anchored the boat about one-hundred yards from the starting line and supplied us with binoculars so we could watch the races. Try to picture a beautiful calm sunny day as we sliced our way through the ocean waters. Spray bounced up but did not dampen the thrill of watching the best sailors in the world maneuver through the dark blue ocean waters.

I had never been on a yacht—never mind during a race of this magnitude. It was exhilarating to watch the beautiful ships fight for position all the while trying to keep steady as waves rocked our own ship. Watching the races under such conditions made me realize just how skilled the captains of these magnificent boats actually were.

I felt a sense of déjà vu the entire day before I realized I was being reminded of my experience at the Grand Prix. I had watched the event while Maurice's attention had been otherwise occupied. In his defense, a yacht had passed by containing a scantily clad woman sunning herself on its deck, something which could distract just about anyone's attention.

After the conclusion of the day's races, Maurice and I made our way to The Farm, a fantastic restaurant where we were served by the monks who owned the establishment. It was situated at the top of the Grand Corniche, a mountain that separates Nice and Monte Carlo. With its picturesque small towns and a dream-like coastline, Grande Corniche rates among the most spectacular roads of Southern Europe and was featured in the opening of

GoldenEye, a James Bond movie. That said, the top of the Grand Corniche is something few people experience because it's at the pinnacle of a terrifying stretch of road that's shaped like a corkscrew. I remember holding on to whatever I could find with my sweaty hands as Maurice drove us up the road. It was worth it though. When we reached the top, the views were breathtaking. We could see Monte Carlo with its basin full of yachts. It was an amazing view of that principality that few people would ever get to enjoy!

When we arrived at The Farm, ordering was quite an experience. I chose the live chicken I wanted for my meal from a pen and before long, they caught and cooked it, along with vegetables picked from a garden right on the premises. We then watched as the monks silently stomped on grapes with their bare feet so as to start the wine making process. They knew how to put on quite a show. A fact that helped make the food and atmosphere heavenly. I guess you could say this was the first "farm to table" restaurant ever.

After eating, Maurice met up with one of the nurses we found on Captain John's yacht and ended up taking her to his apartment in Nice.

That evening, we partied at Juan-les-Pins, a resort town where not a speck of garbage could be found, even though it was known to have a festive atmosphere. There was no other town like it in the world. Loudspeakers blasted music from street light poles, and everywhere I looked, I saw people drinking on the sidewalks. At the time, the town was owned and operated by the teenage children of the ultra-wealthy and was known to only be open from 10 p.m. to 6 a.m. most days of the week during the summer (the only exception being Sundays so people could go to church). I truly enjoyed my time in that one-of-a-kind party town and couldn't help but think that I would have missed out on all of these amazing things if I had ever travelled to the South of France without Maurice. Also, as amazing as all these other places were, my mind kept returning to La Siesta. It was as if I had taken a sip of a forbidden wine and needed more to drink.

Luckily, we returned to that promised land the following night. I floated in behind Maurice, again cutting the line, and again being seated right away by Phillipe, who was clad in an expensive, custom-made suit. When Maurice's head was turned for a moment, I grabbed the man's shirtsleeve and whispered into his ear. "Make sure the check comes to me tonight." Despite the fact that I had been to La Siesta once before, everything still looked strange and new to me, including the torches, the bats, and the way the torchlight bounced off the indoor pool. It was like something from a James Bond film.

As I got my first drink, I heard a song come over the loudspeakers: Serge Gainsbourg's *Je T'aime—My Love*—a song I was told Pope Paul VI tried to get banned throughout Europe because it was too sexy to be played in public. At La Siesta, however, that song was played on a continuous loop, every twenty minutes or so. It is an incredibly sexy tune that features a live female orgasm. As I later discovered, it had an interesting history, one that would serendipitously align with the evening's events. Serge Gainsbourg originally wrote *Je T'aime . . . moi non plus* in order to seduce Brigitte Bardot—who at the time was married to Gunter Sachs, a German businessman.

Brigitte Bardot, late in 1967, was going through a difficult period in her marriage when Serge Gainsbourg became infatuated with her. She agreed to go on a date with him, but on that date, Gainsbourg was so intimidated by Bardot's beauty that he completely lost the wit and charm for which he was well known. Afterwards, Bardot called him and insisted that he write her "the most beautiful love song you can imagine" to make amends for his poor performance. After listening to the song, Bardot headed to a recording studio in Paris with Gainsbourg to record it. According to the sound engineer involved in the recording, Bardot and Gainsbourg engaged in lovemaking during the recording. Apparently, the recording was played just once on Europe 1 radio since Bardot's husband immediately threatened to sue Gainsbourg.

As Maurice and I strolled around the pool, watching girls dance on the metal lily pads sprinkled across the water, we saw a few members of La Siesta's staff line the surface of the pool with rum and throw in a lit match. Flames rushed across the green water, illuminating the patron's faces in glowing amber. I soon learned that the staff did this on an *hourly* basis. Each time they did, the crowd would let out a raucous cheer, and the party atmosphere would ramp up to yet another level of debauchery.

Maurice and I chatted with club goers for a bit and drank wine, enjoying ourselves in the process. There were rumors circulating in the club that Gunter Sachs's yacht was in the harbor and that he and Brigitte Bardot were somewhere in the building. Curiosity piqued, Maurice went on the hunt for Philippe to find out whether there was any truth to the rumors. Maurice loved being where the action was. "Can you take us down to meet the owners?" he asked when we found La Siesta's manager. "I've heard rumors of a secret room downstairs, and I hear there are some VIPs there tonight."

"That's above my pay grade," Philippe responded. "But I'll check."

Philippe came back a few minutes later with a flashlight in his hand, and guided us past the bathrooms, and down a long dark corridor. At the end of the hall was an antique wooden trapdoor. The manager swung the door open and we followed him down a swaying rope ladder. At the bottom, we entered a hidden room. It had marble floors and a huge bar outfitted with hundreds of bottles of top-shelf liquor from all over the world. Music was piped in from above and special romantic lighting glowed suggestively. It was like being in a cave, but one filled with every luxury in the world. I had to use the restroom soon after entering this room and discovered that it itself was the size of a hotel suite.

I came back out of the restroom and discovered that Maurice had quickly gotten into a conversation with the La Siesta owners, three incredibly well-dressed gentlemen which Phillipe had directed him to. They had all moved to a corner of the room. That said, I stood frozen where I was, jaw almost touching the floor. I swear, I was stunned when I saw Brigitte Bardot herself, walking my way, with a humongous smile on her face. She must have felt sorry for me, as my astounded look seemed to make me the immediate recipient of her caring nature. You may not believe me when I tell you this, but when she approached me, she asked, "Would you like to dance with me?" Hell, I must not have believed what was happening because it took me a short while to realize that I hadn't answered her.

"Yes, of course." I responded, when I finally regained the use of my brain. As we danced, she told me she was bored because her husband was always doing business, which could explain why she asked me to dance. She also expressed curiosity about Maurice, who she said looked like a better-looking Omar Sharif, the star of the Academy award winning movie, "Dr. Zavargo." To me, hearing her speak English with a French accent was the sexiest sound in the world. Her eyes beamed out sex. She was immensely friendly and charming, and I kept asking myself whether I was dreaming. When it was my turn to speak, Ms. Bardot listened to me intently. I loved that about her. I talked to her about Maurice and explained that he was a college friend from Iran and that we were driving through Europe for the summer. We continued chitchatting for a few minutes after that. When we broke apart, I floated back to Maurice with a giant dumb grin plastered across my face.

"Maurice, tell me really," I said, "is tonight just a dream?"

His response was so stereotypical of Maurice. "Tonight, is whatever you want it to be, Garree." With that, he gave me his cheeky Maurice wink.

"What have you been doing?" I asked, still trying to catch my breath.

"I was conducting some business with the owners here. Maybe I am more of my father's son than I thought," he said, with a small laugh.

"Maybe so."

"Do you want to get another drink?"

"I don't think it would do much of anything. I'm floating so high as it is."

We left later that night and were halfway home when I remembered that no bill had ever come to me. Either it had been put on Maurice's family's account, or we were living in an alternate reality. Both seemed entirely possible at this juncture.

The next day, I told Maurice that I loved La Siesta so much I wished that we could build one in the U.S.

"What do you think I was talking to the club owners about last night?" he asked, an eyebrow raised. "We were negotiating that for hours. That's why Brigitte Bardot was dancing with you. She was bored!"

Maurice laughed and continued. "You see, I struck a deal where I would give them one hundred thousand dollars for the privilege of duplicating La Siesta. I knew I could get a five-million-dollar interest free loan from my father to get the project started. But, Garree, it must have a casino," he asserted.

"You run the casino, and I'll run the nightclub," I halfway joked.

Boy, did he like that idea! It was actually an idea we had talked about since we started going to La Siesta—such was its power. We did try later on—we came close to buying La Conquistador, a full-blown resort in Puerto Rico at auction—but the Iranian Revolution ended the dream. So, of course, we never did wind end up opening a club of our own, but everything about that fantastic club remains implanted in my memory. I hope my writing does La Siesta justice, as to me, it was like no other place in the world.

Chapter Nineteen

I tried to keep the next day low-key. Nothing could compare to the previous evening anyway. Besides, I knew our trip was heading toward its inevitable end, and I wanted to get some quality time talking with Maurice before that. He was still a mystery to me, after all. That day though, he wasn't in the mood to open up about his past. The only topic he wanted to talk about was *gambling*. Maurice had always said that gambling was in his blood, and in the blood of every Persian.

"The only way I would ever stop gambling, Garree, is if I owned a casino," Maurice told me, as we sipped drinks on our patio and looked out at the ocean. "Then I'd be gambling every day without ever placing a bet." Maurice laughed at his own logic, then suggested we go swap our traveler's checks for cash.

"We'll need plenty of money for the tables tonight," he said, grinning.

I had stopped policing Maurice's gambling at that point and nodded along with his plan. What could I do? Besides, his dad had sent him plenty of money, and he did seem to be on a winning streak again—and he paid me back in full.

Maurice wouldn't let us exchange our money in banks or restaurants, however—we had to go all the way across town to the Money Exchange, where we would get the best bang for our buck. Once there, I handed over my $100 check to the unsmiling woman behind the plastic screen. She handed me back a wad of cash that I instantly knew was too much. A quick calculation showed me that she had given me change for $1,000. Realizing her mistake, I handed the money back to her. Without a word of thanks, she took the money away from me and gave me the correct amount, turning to the next customer as soon as the money had left her hands. I walked away, clutching my measly $100 worth of francs in my hand in frustration. To this day her attitude makes me wish I had taken the money she originally provided me. When we returned a few days later, she didn't even remember me. All I really wanted was a bit of acknowledgment.

Maurice and I had a fair evening at the tables later that day. After deciding we'd had enough of the casino, we walked to the boardwalk for drinks. At the bar, I saw a woman standing alone. I don't like to judge people on looks alone, but let's just say that she was a far cry from Brigitte Bardot. I turned to see Maurice shimmying over to her, a big smile on his face. I ordered three drinks from the bar and went over to the pair. Maurice was already halfway through one of his stories by the time I got to them.

"You see, I am in a predicament. My father has seven wives, my brother has six, but I only have three," he said in an enhanced Persian accent. "I do not want to go back to my country as a disgrace." The woman clearly didn't know whether to laugh or feel sorry for him.

I smiled apologetically to the woman on behalf of Maurice. She returned the smile from under a thick crop of brunette hair, her freckled nose wrinkling as she did so. The three of us spent the next hour talking and laughing, Maurice even confessed that his "wives story" was a load of bull. This made her laugh even harder. She may not have been beautiful, but damn, she was funny. I had no idea why Maurice had decided to bring this woman back to his apartment when he could have chosen any woman in the South of France.

I don't tell this story because I want you to laugh at or think anything negative about this woman. I tell it because I think you will find wisdom in what comes next. To me, wisdom is learning from others and I certainly learned something from Maurice that night. He "entertained" the woman in his bedroom the entire night, and the next morning ordered up a lavish breakfast to the room. The breakfast came from the Negresco Hotel and included six trays of food which were delivered for the three of us. All in all, it cost us $200. She came out of their room afterwards with the biggest smile on her face which was as red as Santa Claus's suit. A short while later, Maurice appeared from the bedroom, and drove the woman back to her hotel room.

Upon his return, I looked at him quizzically and asked, "Are you going to explain to me what happened between you two?"

"Well, Garree," Maurice replied, "When two adults like each other very much . . ."

I couldn't help but laugh at his gall. "I know about the birds and the bees, Maurice."

Maurice paused for a moment and considered the ceiling. "In all honesty, Garree, I made a woman very happy last night. What could be better than that? She needed me way more than the beautiful women out there. She will still remember this night *fifty years* from now."

In that moment, I understood completely what Maurice was saying. He was able to give the woman an experience she otherwise wouldn't have had. She spent the night with a charming and handsome younger man and probably remembers that night to this very day. He refused to judge her as so many other men might have. He simply accepted her for the person she was and treated her like a princess. That's why I always refer to Maurice as a prince. He was always able to make the people around him feel like royalty, no matter who they were. That's real class.

That night, we went to Monte Carlo to gamble. "It's time to play with the big boys," Maurice told me as we drove over. When we arrived, we were told that we had to register our details with them in order to get in, a fact that didn't really bother us too much. While completing my own forms, I happened to notice that Maurice's paperwork stated that he had a credit limit of $1 million, approved by his father.

"Usually, it takes two to three days to get your credit approved here," Maurice told me. "But they'll approve you immediately because of my dad's credit."

Surprisingly enough, the night was uneventful. We gambled, talked to women, and drank, but we ended up leaving the casino early. A good thing too, given what happened the following night.

We spent the next day lounging on the beach in Nice and swimming in the sea. The dry heat that day made us sleepy and happy. All I wanted to do when we got back to our apartment in the early evening was wash the salt and sand off my body, and then have a nap. I had asked Maurice for a night off so I could relax and spend time processing our adventures thus far as I felt my head might literally explode if we took on one more adventure. After rinsing off the remains of the day, I climbed into bed in my underwear, ready to have a couple of hours of sleep. Sunlight was still beaming through the window, so I didn't think I would have a problem waking up later on.

When I jolted awake, the room was pitch black, and I could hear laughter and voices coming from somewhere in the apartment. I reached over and flicked the switch on the lamp, fumbling for my watch to check the time. It was midnight; I had slept for about five hours. Before I had a chance to collect my thoughts and wake up properly, Maurice barged into the room, flinging the door wide open. "Good, you're finally awake!" he shouted across the room. "Follow me, Garree. I've got a surprise for you!" He grabbed my wrist and dragged me from the room, grinning all the while. The harsh light of the living room greeted me, along with two semi-naked women. I realized then that Maurice had purchased us ladies of the night for the evening. I turned on my heels and went back into my room to put on some trousers and a shirt. Maurice was absolutely beside himself, laughing, and still hadn't managed to contain himself when I walked back into the room.

Maurice thrust a beer into my hand a moment later and explained the situation. "These lovely women are ladies of the night whom I hired for the weekend. And since they now have the weekend off, we are all going to spend it together, Garree. What do you think?"

Spurred on by my silence, he continued, "We'll spend the rest of tonight enjoying each other's company and some drinks, and then finish it off in our separate beds. Tomorrow, we will spend the day at the beach, and the evening in La Siesta. If all goes well, we will be able to enjoy each other again when we arrive back from La Siesta." He paused here to wink at the ladies. "Sounds good to you?" The women smiled and nodded in enthusiastic agreement. They were being treated well and didn't have to spend a penny. As it turned out, the weekend worked out even better than Maurice had planned, if you catch my drift.

On Monday morning, after the women had left, I wanted to call home and see how my family was doing as it had been a while since I had heard their voices. Maurice and I went to the post office and asked to use their phone to call a U.S. number. I was told by the phone operator that I would have to wait four to six hours to put the call through, and that I would have to wait patiently. Maurice grinned at me saying, "Don't worry, Garree. Now follow me."

We ended up at a payphone. Maurice picked up the phone, dialed, and passed the receiver to me. In less than thirty seconds, I was talking to my dad.

When I hung up the receiver, I turned towards my friend and asked, "How in the world did you manage to do this?"

"My dad pays Paris Operator 322 five hundred dollars per week to put his calls through quickly. The phone system in Iran is even worse than here." He smiled at having taught me such a valuable lesson. It certainly was one I would not forget!

I'm not ashamed to say that over the next five or so years, I used Paris Operator 322 to place my calls each time I was in Europe. It was a handy little trick.

We celebrated Bastille Day in Nice on July 14th, which just so happened to be Maurice's birthday. Though we spent the day at the beach, that night, I saw a great many people on the boardwalk watching fireworks. I asked Maurice what was happening and he responded by saying, "Celebrating my birthday, of course!" I almost believed him. People seemed to worship him everywhere we went, so why wouldn't they give him fireworks for a day?

Before we left for Europe, we had arranged with our girlfriends to meet them in Majorca, Spain at the end of the summer for one last week of relaxation. Before leaving the Negresco Hotel, we received confirmation letters from our girlfriends saying that they were looking forward to the trip. I was sad to be leaving France, but Maurice promised me it would not be our last visit. As such, I was already eagerly anticipating the next one.

Chapter Twenty

Maurice piloted the Mustang across France to Barcelona, Spain where we would be catching a flight to Majorca. He drove well over the speed limit during one portion of the trip, attracting the attention of gendarme, France's motorbike-riding police. We were instructed to pull over as the police officer caught up to us, but Maurice ignored the order and slammed on the gas. I looked over my shoulder and saw the policeman growing smaller as the Mustang's powerful engine left him in the dust.

"Just what in the hell are you doing?" I asked. "They'll catch up with us at some point."

Maurice took a hard left turn down a side street and slammed on the brakes. "Change seats with me, Garree," he said by way of explanation. "Now!" The urgency in Maurice's voice told me not to question his judgment.

He jumped out of the car, and I slid across into the driver's seat. We pulled off the maneuver just as the gendarme skidded to a halt beside the Mustang and started berating us in French. I spoke no French, but I could tell he was less than pleased with us. Maurice communicated with the policeman in bouts of rapid French, translating to me what he could. He explained to the officer that he was the son of the Iranian Ambassador. The officer did not seem impressed, but Maurice was not fazed. He knew, as he explained to me later, that French gendarmes at the time were known for greasing their own palms with the extra cash from fines. He explained to the gendarme that we would happily pay the fine, but that we only had German marks. The policeman thought this over, then, rather reluctantly, agreed.

Maurice handed him a hundred mark note and was given seventy-five francs as change. Given that francs were worth more than marks, Maurice ended up coming out ahead even after paying the twenty-five mark fine. Maurice was untouchable as always. That accomplished, we once again set off, Maurice waving cheerfully to the policeman as we drove away.

"You want to explain yourself, Maurice?" I demanded as soon as we were out of the gendarme's line of sight.

"I don't have a driving license, Garree," Maurice confessed. "Never needed one." Seeing the shocked expression on my face, he exploded in a fit of laughter. I berated myself internally as I should have known this fact. I had never seen Maurice's nonexistent license, after all, and he had been driving most of the trip!

"Well," I said. "At least the rest of the drive to Barcelona will be uneventful. With you, it's almost *too much* adventure!"

I was almost right. We made it to Barcelona without issue but got lost trying to find the airport. We asked passers-by where it was in our extremely broken Spanish, flapping our arms in wing-like movements to mimic flying. Either they misunderstood our questions, or we misunderstood their directions because we continued to have a terrible time finding the airport.

We arrived there very, very late, panicking about missing our flight. No amount of rushing, however, prevented us from doing so as we soon learned that we had, in fact, missed our flight by several hours. The next flight to

Majorca wasn't until 6 a.m. the next day, fifteen hours later. We knew ourselves well enough to know that it would be best for us to camp out at the airport until then. It turned out that about twenty-five other young people had decided to do the same, so, while Maurice decided to have a nap on top of the empty bar, I had a ball with the other travelers. Moreover, someone had a guitar, so we spent some time listening to music. Before I snuggled down in a sleeping bag with a lovely young lady from Indiana, I asked the guard on duty to make sure we were awake for our flights.

The next morning, the guard very courteously woke us up and we were shortly afterwards finally on our way to Majorca. It dawned on me then that my time with Maurice, as "brothers" alone on the road, was now quickly coming to an end. The time we had spent together in Europe was one I will never ever forget, as it was formative for me as a man in so many ways. I had traveled with a prince, or at least the closest thing to one, and I felt like royalty. But now it was time for us to holiday with our girlfriends from home before heading back to the States. I was sad to leave the Mustang behind, as the car had served us well for 19,980 miles. Maurice explained to me that a broker had been instructed to pick up the car from the airport. This was Flora's doing; it seemed she fancied a change. I didn't blame her. Maurice and I had put a lot of miles on that car, both literally and metaphorically.

Chapter Twenty-One

We arrived in Majorca exhausted, and more than ready for a week of relaxation. I was surprised that the airlines had carried our entire luggage without batting an eyelid as there was quite a lot of it. Though it took some time, we eventually lugged all of our luggage to the beautiful hotel our girlfriends had chosen for us. The hotel was a refurbished castle high up in the mountains with a huge pool, a beautiful terrace for dinner and dancing, and the most breathtaking views. They had chosen well. The girls were due to arrive a short while after us, so Maurice and I went to our separate rooms. As soon as I arrived and put away my luggage, I collapsed into the crisp white bed and slept deeply until my girlfriend, Eileen, burst into the room. Despite everything that had happened on our trip, I had missed her, and we had a lovely reunion in the hotel room.

The four of us spent the week shopping, relaxing by the pool, or horseback riding around the grounds. We also drank more than our fair share of sangria as it was only five dollars for a pitcher. During the stay, I treated Maurice and our girlfriends to a bullfight featuring a great local matador, along with enough sangria to sink a ship. I felt I should be as generous as possible as I wanted to thank Maurice for our trip. The holiday was certainly peaceful, but I was starting to miss the excitement that came with travelling alongside Maurice. The week ended far too quickly and before I knew it, Eileen and I were getting ready to head to the airport to hop on a plane back to the U.S. Maurice's girlfriend did the same, but she was headed home to New York. Maurice, however, was planning on travelling back to the South of France to close Flora's apartment in Nice, then make his way back to London for one final visit with his sister, Flora, before returning to the U.S. himself.

Standing at the hotel waiting for our cab, Maurice and I milled around in a somber manner. It was a sad day for both of us as our travels together were officially over. We'd had so many experiences together over the past few months that it was hard to believe this was the end. Maurice and I embraced before Eileen got into our taxi. He promised me then that this would not be the last time we would see each other outside of American soil.

His parting words to me, in an incredibly elaborate and over-the-top voice, were, "Always shoot for the stars, Garree. That way, even if you only reach the moon, you'll still be way ahead of everyone else."

People were looking at us as we said our farewells, but we didn't care. We parted ways laughing. Maurice and I had decided early on in our trip that we would share an apartment back in Boston. I was quite looking forward to seeing what other adventures that would bring. I entered our taxi and we made our way to the airport.

I realized just how much I had learned from Maurice when we arrived in London to catch our flight back home. The airport staff told me that my luggage was too heavy—as if I didn't already know that—and that the added charge would be £220 for it to be allowed on the plane. The alternative would be to ship my bags to the U.S. onboard a cargo boat. This option would be free, but it could take three months for my property to be returned to me. I tried to argue the price down with the staff members, but they told me they would lose their jobs if they did so. Realizing I was in the middle of a losing battle, I asked to speak to management. Eileen was with me, and we were both escorted to the manager's office.

We sat there in the dingy office, the manager staring belligerently at me. He was smug and cocky. I didn't like him one bit. Meanwhile, I had twenty-five pounds folded up in my right hand, the exact amount of money I was prepared to part with in order to get my luggage on the flight. I explained the situation to the manager, adding that I only had twenty-five pounds to spare. He laughed in my face, telling me that this was not possible. I recalled passing a sign in the hallway stating that student tickets from London to the U.S. were only £199—less than what they wanted to charge me for the additional luggage.

I puffed out my chest and said to the manager, "If you aren't willing to take my offer, then I would like to purchase another seat please. My luggage will ride in style next to me, and your air hostesses had darned well better ask it if it wants some tea or coffee."

At this point, the manager's smug look vanished. He tried to argue that this was against regulations. I then asked for the use of his telephone to ring my lawyer. I was half-way through typing Flora's number into the phone, as hers was the only English telephone number I could remember, when he caved. He would take the twenty-five pounds and put my oversized luggage in the hold. Maurice had taught me well how to bluff, a valuable skill which has come in very handy over the years. I boarded the plane feeling very satisfied. Most of all, I felt pleased by the thought that Maurice would have been proud of me.

Part Three - Real Life

Chapter Twenty-Two

Back home, I was almost relieved at the thought of returning to work. At this point in time, my dad's tire store had never felt more normal to me. Travelling can be hazardous to one's health, especially with someone like Maurice and the insane pace at which he moved. I told myself that what I had experienced simply wasn't real life. Even so, after these dazzling days and nights, coming back to reality might have been challenging to many people, but I welcomed reality with open arms.

As soon as I got home, my mother had quite a story for me. Shortly after I left London, the emerald dress I had seen in Flora's store, which was made for Princess Farrah of Iran, arrived at my mother's doorstep. The dress was made with actual emeralds and was priced at more than $100,000. Interestingly, I had only known Flora for twenty minutes when I had told her, "That dress would look great on my mom!"

The package was addressed to my mother, with an elegant handwritten note from Flora herself.

Dear Mrs. Orleck

I had the pleasure of meeting your son, Gary, on his travels around Europe with my brother. Inside is a gift for you, which Gary chose himself. You've raised a fine young man, Mrs. Orleck.

All my love, Flora.

My mother was speechless when she saw the dress, and even *more* astonished when I told her how much Flora's creations sold for. The dress gave me the opportunity to speak with my mother about Flora and her little family in London. Describing them for her was something I had longed to do but had no idea how much. Now, the thought of Flora writing such a kind note to my mother made me feel incredibly wonderful and appreciative. My mother was also deeply appreciative of the gift, but returned the dress to Flora nonetheless. She wrote her a very nice note back, explaining that while it was a beautiful and generous gift, she "had nowhere to wear something that expensive" and could not, in good conscience, let it gather dust in a closet.

During this time, I had also taken the liberty of sending some photos of my European trip to Maurice's father, who in turn sent me a lengthy thank you letter—one I still have after all these years. His gratitude was important to me because I held him in such high esteem after hearing all of the stories Maurice told me on our trip.

My life fell back into a routine after that, as days slipped by in a mundane blur of work and sleep. Still, I showed as many people as I could photographs from my trip to Europe, as if to remind myself that it was real, that it had definitely happened. What I did not realize was that I had stepped on a metaphorical merry-go-round—one I would not be able to step out of for a long time. It was a merry-go-round that Maurice was on too, both of us rotating around the desire for adventure. If we picked up where we left off, at least I wouldn't be alone on the ride; Maurice would be right there with me.

Not long after arriving back home, I realized that I would need to start working harder. I wanted to be successful, and I needed to quickly replenish the money I had spent on the trip. I wasn't lucky enough to have family money, as Maurice did, so I decided to move back in with my mom and dad.

Shortly after this, Eileen asked me if I was ready to marry her. I thought about it, but decided I wasn't ready for that level of commitment yet. This was a complete 180° turn from my mindset before we left for Europe. Back then, I thought I wanted to be married by twenty-one. I blame Maurice for this change of heart. After I experienced my fair share of women in Europe, I realized that Eileen and I were not meant to be. I was just not ready to settle down anytime soon as I wanted to put my efforts into making something of myself. Eileen soon after decided to go back to college in California. I even drove her to the airport.

Maurice returned to the U.S. about two weeks after I did, and we soon arranged to meet at a basketball game. I'm not ashamed to admit how excited I was to see my "brother" again as I had really been missing him. When you encounter a personality as big as his, you notice when it's absent.

That night, I treated him to dinner, which made him smile. "You haven't changed at all, Garree," he commented as he tucked into his sandwich. "You're still one in a million. You know, I tried renting a two-bedroom apartment in my building so we could live together. Unfortunately, though, they didn't have one available."

Maurice thought for a moment and then looked at me. "Would you sleep on the couch?" he asked earnestly. Since he said he would not take a nickel of rent from me for the use of the couch, this fit my frugal plans perfectly. I gave Maurice duplicate photographs from our trip, and he seemed very pleased with the album. I'm pretty sure he lost it pretty much straight away, but I still felt good having given it to him. Either way, Maurice and I left each other that night renewed in our plans, and in our friendship.

Shortly after the night Maurice and I met up, a letter came from Flora reminding me of my promise to help her find a Cadillac—the exact model Elvis had driven. The envelope contained a cashier's check for $25,000. The letter instructed me to purchase the car and keep the change!

With Flora's request in mind, I spent the next few weekends circling car advertisements in local newspapers and visiting dealerships. I eventually found the right car—a cherry-red 1968 Cadillac convertible. The chrome pieces of the car which glinted in the sunlight gave it an ethereal look. She had the car with her within the next week. This was completely incomprehensible to me: to have this kind of money on hand and be able to spend it on something frivolous was mind-blowing. The truth of it was that Flora was a very successful person, and I believe she wanted to show the world what she had achieved all by herself. That's what the Cadillac meant to her. When daddy's a billionaire, most people would assume the Caddy was bought by daddy. So, for her, it was more than just a car; it was a trophy, a public display of her personal success.

By the way, there was a difference of $5,010 left over from Flora's initial check. I wasn't the type to "keep the change" on a transaction like that, even though she had told me to, so I sent her back the "change."

Flora was very pleased with my purchase on her behalf and invited me to visit her in London any time I wished. This was something I fully intended to take her up on as soon as I got the chance, though life has a crazy habit of getting in the way.

Chapter Twenty-Three

Weeks went by and the days got colder. Soon it was winter, which is the busy season in the tire business. Maurice invited me to go skiing with him, but I was afraid of getting hurt and not being able to work through this heavy time of year. As such, Maurice ended up spending the winter season skiing while I spent it working. But thanks to Maurice, on the weekends, I had the unrestricted use of one of the most prestigious apartments in Boston.

The only thing that irked me about my life at this juncture was the nine-to-five routine. I hated this rigid structure. I particularly hated the early mornings, and in fact, arrived at work late almost every day because of it. This irritated my father, who liked his days to be structured. Needless to say, we butted heads. I coped by trying to have a more active night life. Unfortunately, this led to more late mornings and more arguments with my father.

My arrangement with my father was complex. We had both agreed that he would treat me like any other member of staff, yet I was expected to stay later in the evenings—long after the other workers had gone home. I was also expected to make decisions that no one else would and make sales no one else could. The pressure my father placed on me was relentless. I know he wanted me to succeed, but our relationship grew increasingly strained.

Nevertheless, I did learn many business lessons from my father—lessons only experience could teach you. As a result of my knack for selling, I was assigned to a sales position on the road. Taking advantage of my new position, thankfully away from my father's watchful, prying, and judgmental eyes, I was able to sharpen my selling techniques. For one thing, I refused to carry a price list with me. I wasn't selling the tires—I was selling myself and my brand. I believed that everything else would fall into place once the client wanted to work with me. That said, I have to admit that I probably became "too friendly" with some customers as well as some members of the staff. I enjoyed breaking the rules and social norms of the time. In any case, I became so involved in the business that the year flew by in a haze of work and women—in that order. I did grow up a lot that year thanks to the trip I took with Maurice. I began to feel successful at work and even managed to travel within the U.S. a few times. For instance, I sometimes spent weekends in Cape Cod and Bar Harbor, Maine with Maurice. Sometimes we went with dates, and sometimes it ended up being the two of us. I read a lot of travel books during this time of my life as well, but I was also still eager to learn as much as I could about World War II and my Jewish ancestors. The more I read, the more I ached to visit Israel, the Land of Survivors.

Summer rolled around, and I arranged to treat Maurice to the world-famous Newport Folk Festival. Through deep family connections, I got us seats in the front quadrant where all the big shots sat, and we had one of only six suites at The Newport Country Club. On the second night of the festival, as we got off the elevator and were heading to our room at 2:30 a.m., we saw Bob Dylan and Joan Baez (the headliners of that year's Newport Folk Festival) walk out of the suite next to ours. They seemed to be having some sort of tiff.

"I'm sorry I have to leave," she told him.

"Me too!" he replied in frustration as she headed towards the elevator. He quickly turned and headed back to his room.

I have always had a level of respect for the privacy of the famous, so, as we passed them, I only said, "Thanks for a great show, Mr. Dylan."

"I agree, Sir," Maurice added.

Bob Dylan nodded, stepped into his room, and closed the door. Joan, on the other hand, floated away into the elevator.

When we were inside our own room, Maurice said, "Well, Garree, I am impressed with our seats and accommodations. Thanks! You're one in a million to me." He said it with a huge smile on his face.

"If that's true, you're one in a billion to me," I responded.

That summer, I also took Maurice to Boston Celtic, Boston Red Sox, and Patriots games with exceptional tickets I acquired from my business suppliers. As I did so, I finally felt like maybe I was paying him back a little for all that he had done for me in Europe. Under the bright lights of one particular Boston Red Sox night game at Fenway Park, we decided to talk about our plans for the future.

Maurice planned to travel again that summer, but work prevented me from accompanying him, much to my disappointment. That said, I must have been working incredibly hard because my father, the boss, told me in September that I needed to take a vacation. It was the first and last time he acknowledged my efforts at work. Either way, his acknowledgment felt good. I knew what my destination would be, and I knew I needed to go alone. I'm not sure why I concluded that I needed to travel by myself, but it felt right. I needed to go to Israel, especially to the Avenue of the Righteous, and place a rare plant called The Lion next to the plaque of the butcher who had saved Mortiz's family. The Lion, which had rather large red flowers that were said to be vibrant even in the extreme environment of Israel, is typically seen as representing bravery, so I felt it was quite appropriate. There was also a plant and a plaque for Raoul Wallenberg who saved hundreds of Jews from German death camps. He sadly died at the hands of the Russians. Even Shindler was recognized at the Avenue of the Righteous.

So, I was off again, this time without Maurice. I missed him but knew I had made the right decision. During my first few nights in Israel, I became close to a local taxi driver named Simon who had taken on the role of my personal tour guide. With his help, I was able to visit all of the Jewish historical landmarks, most significantly the Avenue of the Righteous, which was truly inspirational. What was also inspirational—in fact, literally breathtaking—was visiting what is now known as the old Yad Vashem. It encompassed a structure that had a tent-like roof but had no walls. It looked almost barren as I approached it.

Simon warned me as I got closer to, "Hold on tight to the railing before you look over." I acknowledged his warning and did so when I reached it. And good thing too! For when I looked over the railing, I saw six million tiny tile squares and nothing else, a memorial that represented the six million Jews killed in the Holocaust. Taking in that silent sea of squares, my legs literally buckled, and though I held on to the railing, my knees hit the floor. It was both a shocking and deeply moving experience.

I wanted to see some of Israel's most beautiful beaches, so a few days after visiting the Avenue of the Righteous, I booked a trip down to Eilat, a resort town close to the Israeli–Jordanian border. On the flight, I met a lovely young lady who only spoke Hebrew, but that didn't prevent us from having a nice time. I broke the ice by offering her an American cigarette which she readily accepted, but after that, we communicated in smiles, laughs, and gestures. When we landed, I accompanied her to find her brother and his girlfriend. Thank goodness one of them spoke some English.

We managed to arrange to meet up the next evening for drinks at a bar near to where we were both staying. I arrived at the club at the same time as the others did.

Directly across from our table, propped against the wall, were thirteen Israeli made Uzi machine guns, surrounded by twelve young Israeli soldiers, dressed up in their military finery. They were rowdy and having a good time. It took me a couple of drinks before I found the courage to go over and ask them what they were celebrating. As I approached, they all turned to me with friendly smiles. I wasn't sure what I had expected, but it most certainly wasn't that. I was told by one of the older soldiers, possibly only a year or so older than me, that they were remembering the life of a friend.

Their comrade in arms had died at the Zion Gate the previous year. Thirteen soldiers, twelve of whom were in this bar, were instructed to take the gate, and only twelve returned home. Their friend had died in their arms. They were therefore celebrating his life, and his passion for his country. Moreover, they had brought the actual gun that he had died fighting with along with them—an extra gun for their fallen comrade. They said it had taken them over a year to get the paperwork through government channels to allow them this tribute.

We were invited by the soldiers to spend the evening with them and so the lady from the plane, her brother, her brother's girlfriend, and I all decided to do so, albeit anxiously. My lady friend had clearly impressed many of the soldiers, and they were falling all over themselves to talk to her. I could tell she loved all the attention, but her eyes kept drawing back to me. I've got to say, that made me feel pretty great. That said, I was still a bit anxious. These guys were a scary bunch, though they did respect my date's brother, who (as it turned out) was a tank driver in the Israeli army. However, they wanted to show me that they carried two knives on them at all times. I assumed it was to impress me and my date, but I was only partly right. They also wanted to explain why they party so hard. The reason being that they never knew which day would be their last. A soldier even told me, "We do not kiss our girlfriends goodnight. We kiss them *goodbye* because we can be called to war in a minute's notice."

One of the soldiers then took a knife out of his shoe and put it on the table. "We always carry two knives, like we said before. This one, for example, is in case we get captured," he said. "We would rather commit suicide then be tortured."

Later that evening, as I was feeling very merry, an older gentleman came to the table and asked to speak with me privately. Intrigued, I followed him to a quieter part of the bar, away from the raucous laughter of the soldiers. The man told me that he'd overheard me talking about my business. He said he also owned a tire company in Israel called La Harre Tires, which produced tires in Israel to be sold all over the world. The funny thing was, I actually remembered having bought and sold some of his tires. He then asked me if I wanted to be the exclusive distributor for his tires in the U.S. Before I could answer, he handed me his card and walked away.

The rest of the night continued in much the same way as it had before. The soldiers and my guests partied through the night, and we all had the best time. The bar was kept open just for us after closing time had passed, possibly because the owners feared the soldiers' reactions should the flow of alcohol stop. When it came time to pay the bar tab, it turned out that the man with the tire company had already done so on our behalf.

As we parted ways, the soldiers gave each of us a big kiss on each cheek. The woman from the plane and I went to the hotel room I was staying in and made love all night. I came to realize that she chose to give me something special—her virginity—that night. I can still clearly picture her delicate face, glowing in the candlelight of my bedroom.

The next day, we met up with my date's brother and his girlfriend, and all four of us headed down to the beach. We ended up next to a couple with their two young children. The family had a small dinghy with them that they were using to ride around in the water. We had set up our towels not too far from theirs, so they asked us if we would watch their children while they had a quick ride out on their little boat. Of course, we said yes and entertained the children while they went for a quick lap in the dinghy. As they coasted around at the top speed of five miles per hour, the little ten-horsepower motor was surprisingly quiet. They weren't gone for too long, and the children were as good as gold and didn't require much of our attention.

As a result of watching the children's parents ride their dinghy, my attention drifted to the Jordanian flag I could see on the other side of the sea. I had recently started a habit of collecting stamps from each country I visited as a way of tracking my travels. As such, I couldn't pass up a chance to visit as many countries as possible, however briefly, and collect some stamps. We were so close to Jordan that I could actually read a sign saying "Post Office," which looked to be a five-minute walk away from the flag. When they got back, I asked the couple if I could borrow the dinghy and take a quick ride across the sea to Jordan. The couple agreed on one condition—that my friend's brother would drive the boat. That was fine with me since that would allow me to take in the sights on the short drive over.

The entire journey took less than fifteen minutes. Just as we were about to get out of the boat, however, I heard a pinging sound in the water near me. I couldn't see what it was, so I shrugged it off and continued to make my way into the water. Then I heard more pinging sounds, about eight in total. It sounded like somebody was throwing rocks into the water near us. There was no one on the beach in front of us and no other boats, so I had no idea what was causing the noise. It took another few pings and small splashes before my friend's brother realized it was the Jordanian Army, shooting at us. When I looked around to try to find out where the bullets were coming from, I saw four armored vehicles stationed on the hill overlooking the post office, their machine guns leveled at us. My heart was pounding out of my chest with the realization of what was happening. It felt like I couldn't get air into my lungs.

Acting on instinct alone, I pushed the boat around into the direction we had come from, jumped back in, and pulled my friend's brother in with me. He snapped out of the panic-stricken daze he was in, turned the engine on, and powered the boat away as fast as he could. Crawling back to the Israeli beach at a snail's pace was the most excruciating experience of my life. When we finally hit the other side, a sigh of relief left my lips. The second I exhaled, however, I noticed four soldiers running down the beach screaming at me in a language I didn't understand. Behind the soldiers were four Israeli tanks pointing their guns at the Jordanian armored vehicles. The soldiers pointed their guns at us when they reached us and gestured for us to follow them off the beach. Of course, we did as we were asked. You don't mess with people who have guns bigger than your arm.

The soldiers escorted us from the beach onto a cliff path and then into a small tin hut at the apex. The tin hut had only a wooden bench in it, which the soldiers pointed to. Their mannerisms left no question as to what they wanted us to do.

For the moment, they left us alone, cooking in the staggering heat of the hut. A short while later, the guards came back and took my friend's brother away. As he left, he gave me a shrug and a worried smile. Alone in that tin hut, I had plenty of time to think about what had happened. It began to dawn on me how naïve I had been, trying to cross into Jordan from Israel without going through the proper channels. When the soldiers returned to the hut, I was still questioning my shoddy judgment. This time, they were accompanied by a man with medals covering his broad chest. Speaking in English, he offered me a drink of water and told me he was the Colonel in charge of the area.

I felt my body relax. Finally, somebody who could understand me! He told me that he had heard my friend's brother's side of the story, and now it was time for me to tell mine. I told him exactly what had happened, in detail. I told him it was all my fault and that I never thought it would be a problem to just get some stamps from the post office. I could have kicked myself as I was telling the story. My sheer stupidity had become painfully clear. The English-speaking soldier was polite, if a little dumbfounded. He couldn't comprehend how I had made such a monumental mistake.

He said in a measured, slightly patronizing tone, "You could have caused an international incident, maybe even a war." I felt pretty small. I had clearly failed to understand the current tensions in that part of the world. The colonel then continued by saying, "It's really only because I maintain open communication with my Jordanian counterpart that the incident had not progressed further." He sighed and then said, "Stupid Americans." It wasn't said in a nasty way though.

The colonel continued on, "I should probably write this up. But, because you took full responsibility, which frankly I didn't expect an American to do, and you both covered for and showed me that you cared for the Israeli citizens with you, I'm not going to do that. I don't think you need to face a judge in Tel Aviv. It was clearly a huge mistake. I thought that Americans always blamed others and never took responsibility. Since your demeanor impressed me, promise me you will leave here tomorrow, and I will let you off."

"Yes, I understand and agree to your terms. I promise to leave Eilat as soon as I can." Satisfied, he extended his hand for me to shake. Which I did. As I turned to leave, he reminded me to not tell a soul what happened.

I eventually met up with my date, her brother, and his girlfriend. I explained that I had been banned from Eilat by the army, but that everything was ok now. Though I had to leave the area by the next day, at the latest, I wished them all well and thanked them for their company throughout my time here. I stood on the beach at Eilat afterwards, reeling from the whole ordeal I had experienced. I could not believe how quickly one's life could change if one does something incredibly stupid. It was definitely a reminder to always take responsibility for one's mistakes.

Chapter Twenty-Four

After almost causing an international incident in Israel, it was time for a change of scenery. By the time I landed in Athens, Greece I was emotionally drained. I needed some time to relax and acclimate to the new country I was in, so I went to bed early.

The next morning, I woke up refreshed, ready to take on the historic city of Athens. As I got dressed, I paused for a moment, thinking how different things would have been had Maurice been with me. We would probably have slept until noon, then headed straight for the casino in Athens. Well, he was not here, and things were going to be a bit different this time around!

My first stop was the Acropolis, where democracy was born. The Acropolis is a fortress built on a hill high above the city of Athens. Inside it is the Parthenon, a well-preserved building which is 2,460 years old. All in all, I was shocked by its sheer scale and how well preserved it was. I spent the rest of the day touring around the city's significant historical sites. I had also passed a few picturesque restaurants on my wanderings, so I headed back to the heart of the city at around two in the afternoon in search of something good to eat.

Instead of finding something to eat, however, fate intervened. I found the most beautiful young woman sitting on the edge of a fountain. The sun shone through the flowing water, creating dancing shadows that swam across her unhappy face. She looked so sad that I almost felt tears coming from my own eyes as I gazed upon her. I wondered what was troubling her on such a stunning day and in such a lovely place as this.

Something drew me to this woman, something which prevented me from leaving without knowing her story. I waited for a space to open up next to her at the fountain, and then sat as close as I dared. Up close, the juxtaposition of melancholy on such an appealing face was arresting. I offered her a cigarette.

To my delight, she accepted. I tapped the packet on her leg, mimicking one of Maurice's mannerisms. I then offered her the packet before taking one myself. For a second, a smile crossed her face. "Thank you," she said in English. She then lit the cigarette and took a deep drag. Her sad demeanor, however, returned a moment later.

"What made you so upset on such a beautiful day?" I inquired, not really expecting a response.

"My boyfriend and I just broke up," she replied, staring straight ahead. I could see tears clouding her eyes as she spoke. "We had been together for a long time. I'm confused about what my next step should be." She blinked the tears away and looked me in the eye.

I didn't want to push her on the subject, so I asked if she would accompany me to dinner. "I'm starving, and I don't know which restaurants are good here," I said by way of casual invitation.

She seemed hesitant, but I could see her thinking about it. I couldn't let her get away, so I tried one more time. "We can talk about life and its ups and downs," I offered, giving her my best "Maurice" smile.

She sighed a little sigh of resignation and said, "Okay. Follow me." She took me to a lovely small restaurant where she clearly knew the staff, all very friendly people. While we were eating, the woman and I laughed a lot. It was amazing how quickly her attitude changed from the sad girl by the fountain to the life of the party that sat before me. She had one hell of a smile, and a laugh that stopped me in my tracks. After the wonderful meal, she kissed me on the cheek and slipped me a piece of paper with her phone number and her name, Melina, scribbled onto it.

I could not believe my luck and spent the rest of that evening thinking about her. Her cropped chocolate hair, olive skin, and hazel eyes haunted my dreams. Not wanting to seem needy, and being a typical man, I waited a day and a half before calling her. Believe me, it was torture. When I finally worked up the courage to pick up the phone, another woman answered, "I'm so glad you've called!" This made me feel unbelievably good. Melina had told me that she lived with her sister so I was pretty certain that's who I was talking to. Moreover, how Melina's sister responded clearly meant that Melina had told her good things about me.

I waited a little while for Melina to come to the phone and heard the distant sound of two girls giggling. "Hello, Garrry," she purred into the phone. Her accent dragged out the 'r' sound in my name. I loved the exotic way she made it sound. We arranged to meet the following night to go clubbing. I could not have been more thrilled when she ended the call by saying, "See you tomorrow, Garrry." I spent that evening in much the same way as I had the previous one: thinking of Melina. I had never felt like this about somebody that I had known for such a short amount of time.

We met at the fountain the next evening, where I got a gentle kiss on the cheek and a hug.

"I've got something special planned for us, Garrry," she told me as I looked into her olive eyes.

It was indeed a special night as Melina took me to music and dancing clubs all across Athens. One played rock music, another played soul, and so on. The nightclubs were all located at the top floor of every building we visited, the openness of which allowed me to see both the stars themselves as well as the nightlife of Athens. My favorite thing about these clubs was that when you had finished a drink, you were expected to smash your glass into one of the huge fireplaces. I lost count of how many glasses we smashed. Either way, we drank, danced, and kissed the night away beneath the starlit skies of Athens.

A couple of evenings later, Melina took me to a Greek wine festival. For the equivalent of a thirty-dollar entrance fee, you could drink wine to your heart's content, and that is exactly what we did. That said, I did not take my eyes off of Melina the entire evening. We left the festival in the early morning, stupid drunk. In the cab, she told me that I had met her at the perfect time, and that I had helped her realize that her boyfriend was controlling and verbally abusive. Her body leaned against mine in the cab as she asked me if I would see her again that weekend. Her family always had a big meal on Sundays, she explained, and she would love for me to join them. As I snuck my arm around her waist, I told her that as long as she was there, I wouldn't miss it for the world.

I arrived at seven o'clock that Sunday evening, and was escorted inside by Melina, who looked happy but nervous. Inside, her parents and sister waited to meet me. Her mother had cooked a seven course meal and her father had bought a case of Greek wine. Her parents didn't speak English, and I definitely didn't speak Greek, so Melina and her sister translated the conversation for us. About halfway through the courses, Melina's father banged his glass with a spoon and stood up. He began speaking in Greek while looking directly at me, so I knew what he was saying was meant for me. Melina's sister, an English teacher, who was taller and slimmer than her sister, translated his words for me.

"When Melina told us you were Jewish, I could not have been more excited to welcome you into our home. Before World War II, I had a clothing manufacturing company, and my partner was Jewish. He was the greatest man I ever met. When the Nazis invaded, we hid him in the closet, which is behind the chest you see behind me." Melina's father proceeded to step towards the chest and push it aside. He then opened the door to a small, dark, empty room that had a single hanging light bulb. With tears in his eyes he continued, "Four people lived inside here for nearly two years, Garrry." He said my name in much the same way as Melina. "If anyone had found them, we would have all been put to death. We fed them as best we could, usually at midnight with food left over from our meals. If we had started buying extra food, people would have become suspicious."

Melina's father abruptly closed the door, pulled the chest back in place, and sank back down in his chair. He looked at his hands as the room became silent. I could tell Melina's mother was not happy about the story being told, especially around the dinner table.

In the awkward silence, I decided to break the ice. I stood up from my chair and raised my glass. "A toast to a very brave family, who risked their lives to save others." I could tell that this was clearly not a topic broached often in this household and that my respect meant something to them. Before I left the family that evening, I told Melina's father how honored I was that he had decided to share his story with me. "I know, in my heart, that he would have done the same for me and my family," he told me, with Melina translating. After I shook her father's hand and kissed her sister and mother on the cheek Melina walked me to the door. She kissed me at the door with such ferocity that I didn't think she was ever going to let go, which would have been just fine with me.

Our time together was rapidly coming to an end, something both Melina and I knew and accepted. With the end of my trip in sight, we decided to spend a couple of days island hopping. We visited startling white beaches during the day and drank the nights away under the stars. Despite having only known Melina for a few weeks, I was already head over heels for her. I hated the thought of leaving her, but that day was fast approaching.

Before I left, I wanted to show her how special she was to me, so, with the help of her sister, I booked a dinner for us at her favorite restaurant. With the incredible ocean view as our backdrop, we ate an octopus dinner and said our good-byes. We promised to meet up again, and at the end of the evening, we parted ways with another mind-shattering kiss.

On my way back to the United States, I dropped by Flora's place in London. I had not realized how much I had missed being around her until I arrived on her doorstep, on The Street with No Name. She opened the door, sporting the world's most charismatic grin, rivaling that of her brother's. It was lovely to see her again, and I almost managed to forget about Melina for the few days I spent in London.

Flora took advantage of my visit and asked me to pick her up another car when I got back to America. This time she wanted a silver Cadillac, with a black top and interior. She wanted the silver Cadillac to be delivered to the nearest port so it could stay there and be used when she traveled the continent. Of course, I said I would do that for her. I liked the fact that such a strong woman needed me for something.

One other interesting thing happened during my time in London. While having supper with Flora one night, a man entered the restaurant and asked for her. The host led him over to the private corner where Flora and I were seated. He handed her an envelope which contained two sets of keys to a brand new Ferrari convertible, a temporary registration, and a note. The note stated simply,

A divorce present.

From, Uncle John.

As soon as she read the note, her eyes lit up. She then quickly relayed to me what was in the note while grinning excitedly. This was the first time that I heard of the divorce, but it didn't surprise me given all that Maurice had told me. That said, Maurice did fill me in on all that had happened at a later date.

I let Flora pay for supper that night, figuring that she probably owned the restaurant anyway. However, we didn't really finish our meals given how excited she was about the car. We left the restaurant as soon as we could and made our way to her new shiny red Ferrari. She then took me for a ride and traveled at bullet-like speed through the small narrow streets of London. Who else but Maurice's family would get a $70,000 divorce present, from an uncle, no less! At one point, she even stopped the car and asked me if I'd like to drive it. Of course, I said yes. With my heart pounding against my chest, I put it through a stiff test. It was exhilarating, to say the least, but it also made me realize just how unique the family was.

Sadly, I didn't get to spend much time in London, as I had to get back to reality. I had my career waiting for me after all.

Chapter Twenty-Five

I returned home feeling not only relaxed, but wiser than when I had left. I checked in on Maurice, and we decided to meet up for supper in a day or so to talk about our travels. When we did finally meet up for supper, he said, "Garree, I was up to the same old stuff in the South of France. I gambled the nights away in Monte Carlo or danced under the moonlight at La Siesta." Ah, to be back at La Siesta, watching the flames dance across the pool! My heart danced just thinking about it.

"I'm planning on attending a music festival in Woodstock, New York. It's being hyped as a fantastic celebration of peace, love, and music," I told him. "Do you want to come?"

"I'm not sure that's my scene," he replied. "But I'll let you know if I can make it."

"I hope you'll come," I told him. "I miss travelling together, even if it is only to upstate New York."

"You should have come to the South of France," Maurice joked.

My hopes were dashed when Maurice called me a few days later and said,

"Sorry, Garree, I won't be coming to Woodstock. I don't fancy sleeping under the stars in the mud and rain."

"I will miss you my friend," I said, slightly disappointed. My disappointment didn't last too long though as Melina called me soon afterwards and exclaimed, "Surprise! I'm in Boston!"

"What are you doing here?" I asked her, ecstatic with the news.

"Trying to find myself."

"Well, I'm going to a music festival in Woodstock, New York soon. Maybe you could find yourself there."

I also took some time to hang out with Maurice, though surprisingly, it didn't always turn out well. One night, for instance, while Maurice was away on errands and I was alone in his apartment, I took a phone call from a man threatening Maurice. He said they wanted $85,000 by the following Friday or they would do "unspeakable" things to Maurice. The voice on the phone was calm and even which made it all the more terrifying. I paced the apartment until Maurice returned home a couple of hours later.

"What's wrong, Garree?" he asked, reading me like an open book. I quickly relayed to him the details of the phone call. A wave of worry washed over his face for a moment before he could fix his visage. He repeated his usual mantra of "Don't worry, Garree," grabbed the phone from the den, and walked into his bedroom, leaving the door open. I heard him on the phone, speaking quickly.

"Dad. I need a hundred thousand dollars for graduate school. Business. Yes, it'll help. Yes, I'll call Uncle John in New York and tell him where to wire the money. Thank you, Dad."

The conversation was clearly short and to the point, but it really upset me. I could not believe that Maurice had lied to his dad like this. My family values were clearly different seeing as I couldn't even dream of lying to my family. My temper got the better of me, and I stormed over to the bedroom.

"Why would you lie to your dad like that?" I asked him, with a pit in my stomach.

I saw his anger rise as he strode across the room. "You don't know what you're talking about, Garree. It's none of your business. Back off." With that, he pushed past me and left the apartment. I was a bit surprised as I had never seen Maurice react this way before. What I learned later, however, would explain his reaction. Though it took time, Maurice eventually explained that he lied to his father because he was embarrassed to admit to his gambling losses. When he told me about this, I indeed remembered that he had told me earlier on our European trip that his father had once said, "I don't mind you gambling, but I mind you losing." Perhaps he actually said that, but he may well have been joking. Either way, Maurice took it seriously. There, of course, is no guarantee that one can win when gambling, which is why it's called "gambling" in the first place.

Regardless, there's never an excuse or a good reason to lie to a parent. I couldn't believe Maurice behaved like this to his own family. I was angry beyond belief, and our friendship suffered. One has to draw the line somewhere, and to me, there was nothing charming about lying to a parent, especially when it came to Maurice's father, the one person in the world whose love and respect he most wanted.

I left the apartment that night with nothing resolved and moved back home with my mom and dad. I continued to see Maurice afterwards, but our relationship wasn't the same as it had been before. We both avoided the topic of his lies, not wanting to cause more strife in our relationship than there already was. We continued our usual routine of partying and meeting women, but it felt slightly empty, as though we were just going through the motions. I was able to get through this period of time by counting down the days until Melina and I would be going to the festival at Woodstock.

Eventually, that day arrived, and we finally went to Woodstock for our first date. Just as advertised, it was three days of peace, love, and music. Even though we spent those three days in the rain and mud, it was a once-in-a-lifetime experience and we loved it. Along with hordes of others, we watched Jimmy Hendrix play the National Anthem on his electric guitar and then light it on fire. And that's not even mentioning the nearly twenty other bands we watched! Moreover, the hordes of people present had little food and water but remained peaceful and shared what little they had with each other. We, for example, survived by exchanging the eight cases of beer we brought along with us for food. As the festival came to an end, we started walking the ten miles back to our vehicle. Pausing at the top of the hill (which we had previously climbed to enter the area a few days prior), we could see the giant crowd that was clearing out along with us. Melina turned to me and said, "There are not this many people in all of Athens."

"It's certainly something."

"Garree, I have a question for you."

"What's that?"

"What are we doing next weekend?"

I laughed. "Well, I can't promise you another Woodstock, but we'll figure out something."

And we did see each other the next weekend, and the weekend after that. We were falling head over heels for one another.

My relationship with Maurice, however, was not in good standing. Over the next few weeks, Maurice and I continued to grow apart. Our relationship simply stopped being what it had been—that of a pupil and teacher, and that of brothers. Another factor pushing us apart was the fact that Maurice was dating a girl at the time I didn't really get along with. We had an argument about her one day, and I voiced my opinion more than once which caused some friction. I had a habit of interfering in Maurice's plans, from the various times on our trip I attempted to dissuade him from gambling, to sleeping on his couch at inconvenient times, to getting involved in his relationships. It was hard for me to understand what lines I could or could not cross as I felt that Maurice and I were close enough to tell each other everything. Apparently, I was wrong.

Eventually I did grow to like his girlfriend. She was helping Maurice settle down and grow up, and I loved the man he was becoming. However, as soon as I had developed a bond with her, Maurice decided that he was bored and ready to move on. This is when I decided to intervene. I warned the girl that Maurice was planning on ending it, and also warned Maurice to be careful to not hurt her. This caused another huge argument between us which definitely didn't help our strained relationship. We had travelled together throughout Europe for two months without a real falling-out, but I had now pushed Maurice to his limit. He laughed when I told him to be kind in the breakup, told me it was none of my business, and advised me "to leave it the hell alone." After this, we spoke even less. The conversations we did have were terse and punctuated with awkward silences.

Eventually, Melina and I got an apartment of our own. A fact that filled me with joy as I loved waking up with her each morning and getting into bed together again each night. Still, I felt like something was missing as my best friend wasn't there to celebrate my happiness with me. I had loved Maurice as a brother, and as a teacher, but now our friendship had been reduced to the odd supper and phone call. I got the feeling that we were seeing each other out of a sense of duty more than anything else. It was sad and strange to see Maurice, someone so full of life and adventure, under circumstances like these. It felt like we were underwater, thrashing about, unable to swim toward one another.

Shortly after Maurice and I had our falling-out, I got a call from an old friend from college, inviting Melina and me to his wedding. I jumped at the chance since I wanted to show Melina more of my life. At the wedding, I was shocked by how much my old college mates had matured since graduating. Some were married with children; others owned their own businesses. They weren't the boys I had partied with in college. They were men now. It hit me then that nearly three years had flown by since I graduated from college. I thought about my life during those three years and contemplated the bright spots. Meeting Melina was one for sure. But if I was being honest with myself, the best times I had were still those in Europe with Maurice. Though Melina and I had started dancing, as soon as we stopped, I stood on the dance floor for a moment and realized that my trip with Maurice would be one of the greatest things that would *ever* happen to me. It was something almost otherworldly in my mind—something that I could not let go of.

I knew then that I needed to make an effort to fix my relationship with Maurice. I couldn't bear the thought that the glittering world Maurice and I had inhabited would become closed off to me because of a series of small arguments. I had hoped that Maurice and I could stay friends as we grew old together, although I doubted that Maurice would ever truly grow up. Perhaps he would keep me young as I matured in my life with Melina. He could be my portal to the world of fun, recklessness, and nights under the stars. At least, so I hoped! Either way, I knew I needed to reach out to him, or risk a life without fun. Sure, I wanted to be as mature as my classmates, but I also wanted to keep one foot in Maurice's world—an ideal world without consequence or worry.

As soon as Melina and I got back from the wedding, I picked up the phone and called Maurice. When he picked up, I noticed that something had changed in his voice. It had a more serious undertone and I could tell that he genuinely wanted to see me. As such, we arranged to meet for supper the following day.

When I arrived at the restaurant, Maurice was at the bar, chatting up the young, attractive bartender. This made me smile—here was the Maurice I knew. He must have sensed me behind him, because the minute I walked through the door he turned in his barstool. "Garree," he said, the old warmth back in his voice. "It's so good to see you, my brother."

I bought us two drinks and went to sit at a table in one of the room's corners, which was lit by a solitary light fixture above our heads. We slipped into an easy conversation, catching up on things that had happened since we last spoke six or so weeks ago at this point. We did not talk about how he had lied to his father, or about his now ex-girlfriend. I was done meddling in his affairs. I simply wanted my brother back. By the end of the evening, Maurice and I had slipped back into our old ways, with lots of laughter and champagne. It was like we had never been apart.

Life continued on after our meetup. The only difference was that I now had both Melina and Maurice in my life in significant ways. In fact, Maurice and I were getting along so well that he offered to have me join him again on his travels during the upcoming summer, though this time we would stay in the South of France.

"It'll be like old times, us tearing it up out there," I said gleefully.

"Garree, I couldn't think of anyone I would rather go with."

Once summer arrived, the boys were again set loose in Europe. We stayed at Flora's apartment and fell into our old ways, with Maurice gambling as we spent late nights at La Siesta. Days, on the other hand, were spent sunning on the beaches of Cannes, St. Tropez, and Nice.

About a week into the trip, Maurice took off for Monte Carlo alone. He wanted to do some serious gambling and I didn't feel like tagging along. I didn't like to be around him when he went into a serious bout of spending at the tables, and I certainly couldn't keep up with him in the finance department. "I'll be back in two days, Garree," he told me as he slid into the driver's seat of Flora's latest Cadillac. He drove off as I waved goodbye.

I spent my time at the beach, having a drink or two on the terrace, or on the phone with Melina. She was happy I was spending time with my best friend but seemed a little wary of our capacity for amorous adventure. She didn't have anything to worry about though as I was being a loyal partner.

One evening I heard a commotion outside the apartment after 1 a.m., a rarity for such a high-class place. I opened the curtains and peered out of the bedroom window. Below, on the street, I saw a squat older woman shouting at a taxi driver, who appeared to have completely lost his temper. He slammed his fist into the horn, while the plump woman covered her ears and screwed up her tanned face. When she opened her eyes, she saw me in the window and began shouting at me in a language I could not understand.

She gestured for me to come downstairs, so, being a gentleman, I obliged her. Even from that distance, she appeared to be a woman you could not say no to. I exited the building and found her and the taxi driver arguing in rapid, incomprehensible French.

Eventually, I managed to gather that this woman had not paid the taxi driver. Suddenly, on studying her face more closely, the slim cheek bones, the curve of her nose, I realized that she was Maurice's mother. But why hadn't she paid the taxi driver? It wasn't as though Maurice's family was struggling for money. Somehow, through the use of hand gestures and miming, I managed to understand that she owed the taxi driver almost $700, which she didn't have with her. Not wanting Maurice's mother to be further upset, I went up to my apartment and returned to pay the taxi driver. Thank goodness I had the cash on me, as Maurice always advised.

Afterwards, I escorted Maurice's mother to Flora's apartment. When we arrived at the door, she began gesturing wildly saying, "No, no," and pointed to her apartment, which was across the way next door. I had presumed, wrongly, that because she didn't have a handbag with her, or *any* bags for that matter, that she would just stay in Flora's apartment. Oh, how wrong I was. She took me into Flora's apartment, dragged me to her balcony, and then pointed across to her own balcony next door. She then went back inside, pulled two wooden boards out of the utility closet, and set them across the ten-foot gap between the balconies, six floors up.

Turning back to me, she pointed at the boards, gesturing for me to climb across. More scared of the woman in front of me than of the considerable drop, I quickly shimmied across the boards and slid her patio doors open, which were apparently always left unlocked. Then I walked straight through the apartment and opened the front door. Maurice's mother stood there, beaming at me. She grabbed my hand again, dragged me back into her apartment, and began making tea. I didn't have any other choice but to stay there with her. She was a very convincing woman, and I couldn't have argued with her even if I tried.

Over the course of several cups of tea, I managed to understand that she had been travelling on her own, without her husband, for a stay at a "fat farm" in Switzerland. I was amazed at how well I could understand Maurice's mother without having the ability to speak her language. She talked with her entire body, often acting things out. Maurice's mother had convinced her husband that she wanted to go, despite his protestations that her previous "fat farm" retreats had been failures. I wasn't sure whether Maurice's father agreed to let her go because he was scared of the repercussions that would come his way if she did not get her way, much as I was throughout my interactions with her, or because he liked to give his wife what she wanted. Either way, it didn't matter. That said, Maurice's father had some guidelines, due to the fact that she had escaped from her previous experiences. She was not to take any money with her, which would force her to stay put.

Nevertheless, that didn't work out exactly the way Maurice's father had planned. Maurice's mother ended up escaping the fat farm with only the clothes on her back. She had then commandeered a taxi driver to take her all the way from Switzerland to her home in the South of France. I'd wager that the taxi driver had been too fearful to say no to her. She did manage to send a telegram to her husband on her way to the apartment, however, instructing him to send money. Since she couldn't rely on anyone else, she asked me if I would take her to the Western Union tomorrow to collect the money. She knew for certain it would be there. Of course, I agreed. We said goodnight in our own languages and went our separate ways.

The funny thing was that she didn't ask about Maurice, nor did she know where he was. I doubt she realized that he was off gambling in Monte Carlo. Their family clearly didn't operate the way a normal family does. They made the impossible seem normal, as if they were riding through life in a flying convertible car while the rest of us were doomed to walk. It was a certain kind of charmed madness that I was happy to be around. It was like a taste of another world.

The next morning, I bought breakfast for Maurice's mom, or Mrs. E. as I called her, and then took her to pick up her money. Once she had collected the cash, and repaid me for the taxi, she handed me a slip of paper with an address written on it indicating that I needed to drive her there next. The address tuned out to be a uniquely shaped building that stood out like a sore thumb and was a stone's throw from La Siesta. The building screamed wealth and class. Built in the shape of a pyramid, it contained one luxurious penthouse apartment on the top floor, two on the second, and so on with the last floor containing twelve incredible apartments.

Mrs. E. got out of the car and walked straight into the reception area of the building, leaving me trailing at her heels. She occupied herself with the building manager at the front desk for so long that I decided to take a seat in the lounge area. After what seemed like an age, Mrs. E. shouted "Garree" in my general direction. I loved that she said my name in the same way Maurice did.

I walked over to her and while Mrs. E. continued scribbling her signature on various pieces of paper, the manager explained to me what was happening.

"This lady has bought apartment two for herself and her husband and apartment three for her brother-in-law. Wow, I thought to myself, she just signed her name for $200,000 in the blink of an eye She wants to know if you would like apartment four?"

For a minute, I could not understand what this man was asking me. Did she think I could afford an apartment like this, or was she offering to buy it for me? To this day I will never know the answer to that question, though I now believe that she had actually intended to buy it for me. I always knew I was well-liked by Maurice's family because of the respect I had for him. But even so, I couldn't presume that she would buy me a whole apartment at the time this was taking place. I know Maurice told Mrs. E. that I had a tire business, or did he exaggerate and say I owned the entire Goodyear Tire and Rubber Company? Hopefully, he had explained to her that I wasn't rich, or maybe it hadn't come up. Either way, I explained to the manager that I couldn't buy an apartment. He didn't seem bothered in the slightest and neither did Mrs. E. She shrugged her shoulders and winked at me. In that moment, all I could see was Maurice. They looked so alike.

After that, I took Mrs. E. home, and we went our separate ways for the rest of the day. That evening, she came knocking on my door. When I opened it, she grabbed my arm and said, "Come. Garree. La Siesta!" I quickly got changed and followed Mrs. E. out the door.

Of course, I drove us to La Siesta. Mrs. E. did not give me a choice as she walked straight to the car and waited, rather impatiently, for me to open the passenger door for her. I quickly assented as I couldn't find it in my heart to disappoint this amazing woman. When we arrived at the club, Mrs. E. waited, again, for me to open the passenger car door for her. We then walked to the club arm in arm. After I asked for Philippe, we were guided into the best table in the restaurant overlooking the water. He knew Mrs. E. well after all.

At one point, they brought her steak and it wasn't cooked right. She let out a shriek and they came running to her side. That's the kind of influence she had! All in all, we had a fantastic night dancing and laughing. I paid for all of her food and drinks that night as I felt so grateful to her for giving me Maurice. That might sound strange, but I really did feel that way. She had brought him into the world, and without him, I would have continued to live a sheltered life. I owed her everything. We parted ways at the end of the evening with smiles and a kiss on the cheek. She left for home the next day, and I was left feeling grateful to have had the opportunity to have known her. She was really one fascinating and very strong-willed woman.

When Maurice returned from Monte Carlo a few days later he laughed at the story. "Oh, Garree," he said, "That is just like my mother. She is always breaking out of those places as soon as she gets in them. She never loses a pound. Thank you for taking care of her. Like I always say, 'You one in a million.'"

"She reminds me of you," I told him. "She likes to enjoy herself."

"What can I say?" he replied. "I am my mother's son."

We returned home about a week later. This trip we took together had fully restored my confidence in our friendship, but I had missed Melina terribly and couldn't wait to see her again. When I returned home, we rushed into each other's arms like I was returning from war.

A few weeks later, however, I caused irreparable damage to our relationship. One day, Maurice asked me to bring my Corvette, the 'Vette, as he liked to call it, to his apartment. I didn't think anything of it. When I arrived, a party was in full swing. His living room was crammed full of beautiful women and a couple of happy looking men.

"Garree," Maurice said in a faux-serious tone when he saw me. "These lovely ladies are huge 'Vette fans. I told them all about your car." He gestured toward two fine-looking women who stood giggling in the corner of the room. "Want to take them for a spin?" He winked at me.

Melina and I were very happy together so I had no intention of pursuing these women. I'm not sure if they were aware of that, but it's just how it was. That said, I realized that I had accidentally picked up some of Maurice's flirty mannerisms through the power of assimilation, which the girls seemed to like. We got into my Corvette and I took them for a spin around the block. It was about 3 p.m. when I noticed Melina's car in the parking lot of a store. My heart dropped upon seeing her car because I knew I was in for a rough ride. I parked the Corvette across the street and looked around for her.

Melina came out of the store a moment later, her arms laden with groceries. She recognized my red corvette as soon as she saw it and then looked up at me. Our eyes met across the parking lot, and as soon as she realized what was happening, her eyes filled with hate. If looks could kill, I would have been dead. She turned on her heels and walked as quickly as she could in the other direction.

"I'll be right back," I shouted to my passengers as I got out of my car. My passengers looked at each other, clearly confused.

I eventually caught up with Melina. "Hey wait up," I said. "I'm sorry about those girls in the car. Maurice just wanted me to take them for a spin. You know how he gets."

Melina turned to me and looked at me with an odd expression. "It's my birthday, you bastard," she said quietly. A disappointed look crossed her face as she changed direction, pushed past me and headed to her car. My heart dropped to my knees. Of all the things to forget! She had been such an angel, moving to the States for me, uprooting her life. I tried to follow her to her car, but she slammed the door and sped away.

I got back in my car and took the women back to Maurice's. It was a silent ride; they didn't seem too pleased with me either. After I dropped them off, I went back to the apartment Melina and I shared. She was sitting on the sofa, staring out of the window. "Melina please . . ." I started to say, but she interrupted me.

"Get your things, Garrry." She never took her eyes from the window as she spoke.

"Can't we talk about this?" I asked.

"There is nothing to say."

"Melina . . . I . . ."

"I said get your things, Garrry."

I carried my few possessions out to my car. She was so strong. Once she decided something, there was no changing her mind. I was absolutely heartbroken. I never forgot any of my subsequent partners' birthdays—that's for sure. Heartbroken and disgusted with myself, I headed back to my parents' home, where I was always welcome. My mother reacted exactly as you might expect from a Jewish mother. She was completely overbearing, but full of love. I needed her at that moment, and she was there for her son.

Chapter Twenty-Six

After Melina left, I was really depressed and relied on Maurice's friendship more than ever. To his credit, he was as princely as always, even as I moped around.

"Cheer up, Garree," he would tell me over drinks or dinner. "It does no good to worry."

During this tough period of my life, my friendship with Maurice was very important to me. Over the course of our friendship, he had shown me many new things. I always felt as though I owed him something but also that I didn't have much to give. What do you give a man who has the keys to the world? Then early one evening, I got an unexpected phone call from Maurice that gave me a chance to return a lifetime of favors.

"Hello, Garree. Don't worry, it's okay, but I need you to help me with something. You said you had a connection with the mob. Is this correct?" As always, his voice was completely calm, as though what he was about to say next was completely normal. "Could you get me a driving license please? The cost doesn't matter to me, just as long as I get one. I'm in a bit of trouble."

Maurice's version of a "bit of trouble" turned out to be that he'd been arrested. Over the years that he'd lived in Boston, Maurice had developed quite a reputation for his inability to follow parking restrictions. As a result, there was now a warrant out in his name for multiple unpaid tickets. And when I say "multiple," I mean hundreds. I knew he'd never paid much attention to parking restrictions. In fact, he had a collection of parking tickets that he was quite proud of. But his parking antics had finally caught up with him when he'd parked his car in a no-parking zone at the Boston Airport. The car was parked there for six weeks while Maurice went on vacation to the South of France.

When the police found his car at the airport, they'd hit the jackpot. Usually, they just towed his cars away. This was a minor inconvenience to Maurice as he would just go out and buy a new car. This time, however, instead of towing the car, they stationed a state trooper to stand guard. They had had enough of Maurice's scofflaw tendencies. When he arrived back in Boston, Maurice asked the state trooper why he was standing next to his car. He was promptly arrested.

Upon his arrest, the police started suspecting that Maurice didn't have a driver's license. He had been unable to produce it and during questioning wasn't exactly forthcoming. Maurice was told that if he didn't have a license and had been driving in the States without one for all this time, his visa would have to be reassessed because this was a serious offense. Moreover, in addition to the hundreds of other parking violations Maurice had, the police now suspected that many of the unclaimed cars in the pound were his. How he managed to keep a straight face telling me all of this I'll never know. Of course, he'd been able to post bail. I'd been the first person he'd called after getting out of jail.

Maurice's Iranian lawyer had met him in person and told him that he'd better get a license, and fast. I did have a few connections in the Mafia at that time, which Maurice knew about. That said, I wasn't involved with them at all. They were just guys I had grown up with. What Maurice didn't know, however, was that one of the top Mafia bosses' sons owed me a favor.

You see, in my senior year of high school, two of my classmates and I put up money and built a Corvette with a Bonneville engine to race at the Charleston Dragway in Rhode Island. During this time, Ray Patriaca Jr. invited me to his parties (mostly so I could bring Jewish girls) every Friday night his parents went out of town for the weekend. They were among the few parents that could afford to do so (usually twice a month). Ray Jr. and I became friends during this time, and I even had supper once or twice at his house, though I was too naïve to know that the big black car in front of the house held two bodyguards with tommy guns under their raincoats. Strange too was the fact that when I went to the bathroom, I found a man sitting in a chair in the hallway behind the dining room wall with an object covered over by a raincoat.

Ray Jr.'s father bought him a brand-new Mustang, but it was a four cylinder which we called "a girly car" behind his back. He had purchased this car for Ray Jr. because the son of one of his good friends had died during a racing accident and he didn't want his son to have the same fate. He had, furthermore, expressly forbidden his son to race. Either way, Ray Jr. paid for a third of the car and did work to help us so my other classmate and I didn't mind. We just felt bad for him. As we were wrapping up to go home one night, I asked the attendees of the starting lights we were using to start races to stay a few extra minutes so my friend, who would not be racing anybody, could be timed. Surprisingly, Ray Jr. did well at about 86 mph, even though we had already beat that time by doing 101 mph in a quarter of a mile. Ray Jr. came over to me afterwards, beaming with exhilaration and said, "Gary, I owe you one." His tone then took a more serious tone as he explained, "You better hope my father does not find out I raced your car 'cause he may have your legs broken."

I answered by saying, "Well then, don't let him find out. I enjoy my legs just the way they are!"

Either way, I was calling in my favor. I called my friend and got straight to the point, explaining what had happened to Maurice.

"Money is no object," I told him.

"Okay, if you say so," he replied, tight-lipped.

"Well, can you do it?" I asked, a bit anxiously.

"I owe you, don't I? Anyway, yes, I can help you sort this out," he said.

"Thank you! Could you please have the license back-dated so it could be perceived as possibly being lost in the mail?" I asked, hoping I wasn't going overboard in my requests.

"I'll call you back in five minutes," he responded.

When he called, he said "Have your guy be at the Registry downstairs at the license division tomorrow at exactly 12:00 p.m.—not 11:59 or 12:01 but exactly at noon. Ask for Ray and do not speak unless spoken to. I'll be back in touch with you after that." He then hung up without saying good-bye!

I told Maurice to be at the Rhode Island registry exactly at noon so as to take a photo for the license. That was probably the only time in his life that Maurice was somewhere on time. Two days later, it was delivered to me at my business in an envelope. I told Maurice to come over, and though he did, he elected to stay in his car. I walked towards his car, entered it, and gave him the envelope. When Maurice and I opened it a moment later, it contained a license, dating back two years, and a handwritten note.

> Here is your license, at no cost to you. You will need to return it to me every two years for it to be renewed, or you can kiss it goodbye. There are no games here. It was reported lost two years ago. That is on record. See you soon.

There were no names, no signature, but of course I knew who it was from. As an aside, three years later I got a call. "Gary? Junior here. My dad just bought a limo. It will be in your place of business tomorrow for four new tires. No bill." He quickly hung up. It was then that I remembered that you "owed Them" for every favor asked, no matter what. That said, I still got off easy at $500!

Anyway, the second he saw the license I could see Maurice relax into his seat. I was happy that Maurice would not lose his visa, but I was even happier that I had been able to do something for him. He probably didn't see it this way, since he always viewed our friendship as reciprocal, but it was a big deal to me. Plus, if he got sent back to Iran, he would have been in big trouble, since, as it turned out, he had dodged his mandatory military service there.

Another reason I was glad that I was able to help Maurice with this problem was because we actually went our separate ways for a while after that. Life had simply gotten in the way again. He became busy travelling the world while I became busy with work. We kept in contact as much as possible during this period of time, but it was difficult given that he was almost never home. From what I could gather, Maurice's life remained the same: travelling, girls, and working on family business. If only life would have remained this simple.

Chapter Twenty-Seven

I still remember the day when I saw the news headlines. It was September 16, 1978. *"Thousands Dead in Iran Earthquake."* I was sitting at my kitchen table, an untouched bowl of cereal in front of me. When I read the paper, I nearly choked. My body felt cold as I racked my brain, trying to remember where in the world Maurice was at the time. I knew he was traveling but couldn't remember exactly where he was. Was his family in Iran? Dear God, I hoped they were also traveling.

I tried to call Maurice's parents' house in Iran but was told by the operator that due to the earthquake, it could be two to three weeks before calls could be put through. Her tone suggested that I should have realized that the country was in an emergency. I still had no idea where Maurice would be and no contact information. I realized I had no other choice but to sit and wait. That said, I was pulling my hair out by the time Maurice called me two weeks later.

"Garree!" he shouted down the phone line and into my ear, "My dad bought an apartment building in Boston and he's asked me to manage it. It's more of a phantom job, but you know what that means, right? I get to extend my visa. I can stay in the U.S.! You want to know something crazy, Garree? It's the biggest cash purchase that's ever been made in the history of Boston. One million two hundred thousand dollars, Garree!"

Interestingly, Maurice never once in the conversation brought up the earthquake that had killed thousands of his countrymen and had caused me to panic. I did know that the prospect of potentially having to leave America because of visa issues had been playing on his mind since finishing college, but now he barely let me get a word in edgewise. He was so excited by the news of his father's new real estate acquisition.

Then, all of a sudden, his tone of voice changed, and he became serious. "Come see me on Sunday, Garree. We need to talk about something face to face." I agreed, of course. We made our arrangements and hung up the phone.

When Sunday arrived, I learned that Maurice had been given his pick of apartments. Unsurprisingly, he chose the penthouse. Could you imagine Maurice in anything else? With panoramic views of Boston and ultra-modern fixtures, the apartment suited Maurice perfectly.

When I arrived, Maurice had breakfast ready for us. We sat at his kitchen table for a few minutes, eating the croissants and fresh fruit spread he had laid out. Once we finished and the table was cleared, Maurice turned to me and said, "Garree, I have a question to ask you. My dad really wanted to ask you himself, but he was too nervous to leave Iran. There's a lot going on there at the moment politically. As such, he wanted me to show you this first." Walking us over to his spare bedroom, we stopped at a dining room table which was completely covered by a 3D architectural model of a city. It stood out like a sore thumb as it was blue and white in color. Maurice then turned to me and said, "What you see costs more than you will earn in your lifetime."

He paused to let that sink in, and then he continued. "You're looking at my father's dream, Garree. This is a city my father intends to build in Israel for the Jewish community. It will be a place of refuge, a place of safety. Iran is not so safe anymore for our Jewish people. The anti-Semitic views sweeping across the country are putting the people in danger."

He let me look over the plans for a while as he realized that it was an awful lot for me to take in. As I mulled things over, I couldn't resist touching the smooth hard plastic of the models.

Maurice interrupted my thoughts after a few minutes had passed. "What do you think, Garree?"

To be honest, I'm pretty sure I just blinked at him, a confused look on my face. I was dumbstruck. Surely Maurice's father didn't plan on building an entire city? I knew how wealthy his family was, but was anybody *this* wealthy?

"Wait a minute," I responded, "You can't possibly be suggesting that your father wants to build an entire city in Israel and move the entire Jewish population of approximately 75,000 from Iran to that city?"

"That is *exactly* what I'm suggesting," Maurice answered. His signature smile crept across his face. "These blueprints alone cost more than you'll ever make in your life."

After watching me pace around the room a while longer he said, "It would be his own city, Garree. His own police. His own electricity, bowling alleys, movie theatres. You name it."

I walked back into the kitchen, poured myself a scotch, and drank it quickly. Then I poured another and walked back to the bedroom. "You're telling me this is a *city*, Maurice? This is real?"

"Yes, Garree. It's real. It will cost eight billion dollars, but it will be worth it for all those people to feel safe and have a home. The architect designing all this is one of the best. My father is probably talking to the Israeli government as we speak."

Can you imagine being rich enough to commit to build a city in order to move 75,000 Jews to Israel, plus give a stipend to each person at your own expense? Few people, if any, besides me are aware of how close this came to not being a dream but rather becoming a reality!

"Why are you telling me this, Maurice?" I asked, still trying to focus on all of what Maurice had said.

"Well, Garree. Please bear with me. I'll get to that. But first you need to know a bit more about what this means to my father. Can I continue? Okay. My father is Iranian first and foremost, you know that. But all his children are different. They live elsewhere. He has a helicopter on his roof in case he needs to leave Iran quickly, which he well could. Things are so unstable there. The people are not safe. He used his helicopter for the earthquakes, to help rescue people. He's donated millions in supplies to those affected. He is doing all he can. But he doesn't feel it is enough."

Maurice paused to let my brain digest the information he was relaying, then continued. "Everything he earns is invested immediately. Anywhere but in Iran. He does not want notoriety or fame. He wants to make people happy. Building this city would be a challenge for him, so he needs somebody who can help him do this—under the radar. This is where *you* come in. My father has heard of you, from me and many others, my sisters included. He asked me to invite you to help him. If it wouldn't hurt your family too much, you would need to leave the tire business. He knows you are the most trustworthy person around. Garree, my father wants you to be a purchasing agent. You would travel the world purchasing the best supplies for him, everything from cement to electrical equipment. He wants to pay you $300,000 up front, $100,000 a year, and $300,000 on completion. You'll also get a Gold American Express for charging all your expenses. Pretty great deal. What do you think, Garree?"

I needed another drink. I couldn't believe what Maurice was proposing to me. Nine hundred thousand dollars to travel the world and source supplies to build an entire new city. Surely, I had misunderstood him. I turned and walked back to the kitchen, where I topped up my glass, then sank down onto one of Maurice's plush sofas.

Maurice plunked himself down beside me. He brought the bottle of scotch with him, which I felt was a good idea. "A letter is on its way to you from my father, Garree, explaining what I have just told you. Probably in more detail than I could manage. Take your time, Garree. He doesn't need an answer right away. I know it's a huge decision for you. Just promise me you'll think about it."

"Why don't *you* do it, Maurice?" I asked after a long while.

"I can't do that, Garree. I want to do my own thing. To be my own person. The thought of being in my father's shadow yet again makes me shake. I can't do that. I've seen firsthand what you've gone through with your father, and how a father and son relationship can become degrading. I don't want that." His gaze fell to the floor. You could clearly see he was struggling with the thought. "Please stay for lunch with me, Garree. I promise I won't talk about this anymore." I agreed. I had missed spending time with Maurice. It was my day off anyway and what else was I going to do after being given all of this information?

When it was time for me to leave, I said to Maurice what I had been turning over in my head all day. I needed to make sure I worded it in the right way. The last thing I wanted to do was to seem ungrateful and hurt Maurice and his family. "Maurice," I began, "Of course, I will think of all that you offered. But I don't want to be bought or sold. I'm just a guy from Pawtucket with a little tire business. What do I know of all the things your father wants me to do? I really need some time to think, Maurice. Do you understand that?"

"Don't worry, Garree. Everything will work out. But please think about it. My father wanted someone who is honest, who will not rip him off, and that is why he chose you. It would be the chance of a lifetime for you."

With a brief hug, we parted.

I gave the proposal a hell of a lot of thought over the next month or so, especially when I was having grief at work, which was happening far more often at that time. I felt like I was in charge of nothing, yet in my father's eyes, anything that went wrong was *my* fault. This might sound petty to you, but it was beginning to get me down. When the days were terrible, I often dreamt of exploring a foreign land. In times like this though, I had to check myself. If I accepted the job from Maurice's dad, there would be no time for exploring the world. It would not be glamorous. It would mean living out of a suitcase for three years.

Eventually, I made up my mind to tell Maurice's father that I could not accept. This might seem crazy to you, but despite having a tough time at work, I did love my job. I knew it well, and I was good at it. I was *comfortable* there. How could I guarantee the honesty of others if I had to use languages I did not know while traveling all over the world? Accepting the offer would mean throwing myself into the deep end of something about which I knew absolutely nothing. The thought of leaving the family business to go and work for another family, building their dream, was something I didn't feel I could do. It just felt wrong to me.

Another reason for my decision was that I couldn't handle the extremes that the job would offer. I had been invited to visit Iran many times, but each time I declined. The stories Maurice had told me about the dichotomy of the country—people eating from solid gold plates whilst others starved—made me sick to my stomach. I couldn't be around that kind of injustice. I couldn't be a part of it. I also truly didn't like the idea of the language barrier. After remembering the stories I was told about how the Shah was duped by his friends, how could I know whether interpreters and colleagues would be doing the same to me? Furthermore, if I didn't know the language of all the countries I needed to visit to obtain supplies, I wouldn't even be able to trust the interpreters given that they themselves might be related to the people who were trying to sell me what I needed. The language barrier I would have to face on a daily basis terrified me and made this one of, if not the biggest of the reasons I said no.

It is not that I disliked rich people given that my best friend, my "adopted brother," was from an insanely wealthy family. Rather, it was that I disliked rich people who do not help others, people who create walls around themselves and ignore the strife taking place on their doorstep. Maurice's family wasn't like that. His father, in particular, did all he could to help others. But taking on this role for Maurice's dad would land me knee deep in a country full of selfish wealthy people. I could not deal with that. So, in the end, I chose to decline.

Chapter Twenty-Eight

After breaking the news to Maurice and his father, I decided I needed to get on with my life. They had both understandably been disappointed but understood my reasons. If anything, I think they respected me more for that decision.

As time went by, I at long last moved into a place of my own. I enjoyed the freedom for a while but started to miss being in a relationship. As luck would have it, a friend of mine said she knew just the gal for me. And boy was she right! I was set up with Ronna pretty quickly, and the second I laid eyes on her, I knew she was the one for me.

We met at Flicks, my old haunt. My friend and I sat at the bar while Ronna played pool not far from where we were sitting. My friend knew Ronna, my future wife, and asked if I wanted to be introduced to her. Of course, I said yes straight away, and we headed over. I politely said hello to Ronna and the woman she was playing pool with. When I heard Ronna laugh, I again knew she was the one. Ronna was chatting to my friend and had thrown her head back and laughed at something or other. I was infatuated from then on. I managed to weasel my way into their conversation and was quickly welcomed. Ronna taught Hebrew at a local school and agreed to teach me the language. I warned her that she had her work cut out for her, joking that I barely spoke English. This made her laugh. I felt insanely proud of myself for making her laugh.

I will never forget our first date. After spending the evening at a restaurant, talking and laughing, I dropped her back off at her parents' house and walked her to her door. I was hoping for a kiss. I felt like the night had gone well enough for that. Ronna clearly felt differently. She gave me a hug, thanked me for the date, and went back inside. On my way back to the car I decided I needed to do everything in my power to make her kiss me on our next date. Thinking quickly, and trying to be romantic, I pulled out a business card from my pocket and wrote on the back, "Call me when you're ready for a goodnight kiss. I feel like you owe me." I was over the moon that this in fact worked. She still carries that card in her wallet today as a memento of those days.

Ronna and I took it slow and steady from then on. I didn't want to make her rush into anything she wasn't ready for, as she was only twenty-one years old. During this time, my father and I went to the '73 Super bowl in Los Angeles. He had been rather demanding and grumpy with me at around this time, but he knew how much I loved football. As such, we decided to start the process of repairing our relationship by going to the game together. When the game was over, and we started to leave, I heard "Hello, Garree! Bill!" Who did I see strolling over to our seats but Maurice! The last time I had seen him was when I told him I couldn't accept his father's job nearly a year prior. He had been travelling since then, as he always seemed to be. Aware of the rush of joy I felt when I saw his grin, I ran over to him, dragging my dad along with me. We talked for a little while before he had to rush off explaining that he had a plane to catch. Once Maurice had gone, my father turned to me and actually started complimenting my friend and saying he was a class act. This compliment made me grateful since my father could, at times, be mean-spirited about my friends and other people.

Years later, when I thought about that brief meeting, I suddenly recalled Maurice saying to me, in a kind of odd way, "Oh I see you're still with your dad." The oddness was that I had detected a hint of sadness and envy—not just from his words, but also in his facial expression. Maurice had always tried to please his remote father and clearly had yearned for a father and son closeness that was never meant to be. Yes, he had all the luxuries of the world handed to him (including years at an exclusive boarding school, years at the best private high school, and the ability to spend summers in the South of France), but he was never able to get a close relationship with the father he worshiped and only wanted to please. It was something we always had in common.

Over time, Ronna and I became increasingly serious. We had gotten to know each other really well, and it wasn't long before we talked about taking a trip together. We decided on Israel as it seemed like the obvious choice. Once there, we spent the mornings lounging in bed together and the afternoons seeing the sights. It was like a dream.

We eventually decided to extend the trip and headed for Rome and the South of France. I was so excited to show Ronna all of the glamour this area of the world had to offer. As coincidence would have it, we ran into Maurice and his future wife in La Siesta. I heard his laugh before I saw him, his face glowing under the lit torches. His beautiful wife-to-be sat straight backed, almost regal, next to him. Maurice was holding court with six or seven others, all of whom were doting on his every word.

Maurice immediately broke out of this audience of people listening to him when he saw me and ran over to us. "Garree!" he screamed at me over the din of the modern music, as he dove in for a bear hug. Then he pushed me aside, kissed Ronna's hand, and asked, "And who is this lovely young lady?"

"Maurice, this is Ronna, my girlfriend," I told him.

Ronna knew of Maurice but had not had the pleasure of meeting him in the flesh until now. It was quite nerve-wracking, introducing a girlfriend to Maurice. I was always a bit afraid that they might fall in love with him instead. Luckily, Ronna's attention remained with me after I introduced the two.

"Wow, Garree, she's a bit out of your league, isn't she?" Maurice said with a wink, always the flirt. He then introduced us to his wife-to-be as the people who had been previously listening to Maurice politely scattered. Maurice, his girlfriend, Ronna, and I then spent the rest of the evening together, drinking and dancing. It was the best evening of the trip so far, although I might be a little biased. I think Ronna agreed. For the record, it did feel quite different to be at La Siesta with Ronna, the love of my life, as opposed to seeing it for the first time on my extended European road trip with Maurice. I was thrilled to share it with Ronna, though I couldn't help but compare it to my past experiences. Understandably, I felt a sense of loss. Especially of my carefree youth, and the intensity I felt when I first experienced La Siesta with this Persian Prince, a free spirit who was everything I aspired to be and was not, a character so above and beyond that he left his imprint on me forever. We were older now, and what we had shared before was now a memory.

Maurice then beamed at Ronna and I, saying, "I now live in Condo, which is in London. I even have an apartment in New York City, and a hotel room at the Beverly Wilshire Hotel in Los Angeles for when I conduct business in California."

Maurice and I clinked our glasses together, and he toasted to our evening together with his signature toast, "Here's to those who wish us well, and all the rest may go to hell!" The ladies clinked their glasses together, smiling brightly. Who knew that more than twenty years later, I would be making this same toast in a Boston bar as I mourned his passing?

When Maurice and his fiancée decided to leave, I tried to pay the check but was told that Maurice had already paid it. Knowing I would be upset, he turned to me and said "We will do this again, ok Garree? And I'll let you pick up the check tomorrow night."

Ronna and I decided to spend a few more hours basking in the ambiance of the exclusive club, but I was fuming. As we left, I quickly made my way to my car. Ronna, meanwhile, tried to keep pace with me while asking me why I was so angry. When I eventually calmed down, I explained to her the relationship I had with both Maurice and money in general. I don't think she ever quite grasped what paying for myself meant for me, but she sympathized, and that was enough for me.

When we arrived back at the hotel, a note had been left with the concierge. *"We departed sooner than I thought. Off to a party in Ibiza, Spain with my cousins. Bye Gary."*

The unwritten meaning behind this was clear to me, *"You will never get the check, Garree. I won't give you the chance."* Furthermore, the message clearly meant that he already knew he had plans for the next evening when he told me I could pick up the check for our next rendezvous. I was sad that Maurice had left without giving me the chance to pay him back, but that was just his way with me.

From the South of France, Ronna and I headed to the Italian Riviera, then Spain, and then back to France. When we came back to France, we decided to visit Paris where I excitedly showed Ronna the typical tourist spots of the city and beyond. We also took as much time as possible to simply relax as we enjoyed each other's company. Before I knew it, it was time to go home.

When Ronna moved out of her parent's house and into an apartment with a girlfriend, we fell into a routine. I was almost jealous of the relationship Ronna had with her friend, knowing that I had once been that close with Maurice, whom I now never saw anymore. Work became the biggest part of my life during this period of time. That said, while I often worked fifty-five hours a week, I was able to spend the rest of my time with Ronna. I was nervous when it came to committing to her, especially since I had never committed to anyone or anything else in my life. She had even started discussing marriage with me at some point during this period of time, and that scared the hell out of me. I didn't want to lose her, but she had plenty of others interested in marrying her. I eventually decided that I had better hurry up and marry Ronna so I worked up the courage to ask her. Thankfully she said, "Yes."

Not long after Ronna and I got married, my father and I had another falling out which saw both of our tempers finally boil over. As a result, I simultaneously quit my job and was fired. Ronna and I took this as an opportunity to travel around the United States together. Every cloud has a silver lining, right?

When we returned from the trip, I applied for and began collecting unemployment checks for the first time in my life. Even though my father needed me back to keep the business running smoothly, it took a few months for my relationship with my father to improve to a point where I was able to work my way back into the company and stop cashing unemployment checks.

Life continued on, as it does. Ronna and I eventually bought our first house, travelled around Asia, and then suffered through miscarriages and fertility issues. I called Maurice's cousin one day to catch up and found out from him that Maurice's father never built the city he wanted so desperately to build. Again, I truly believe only I knew how close it had come for the city to actually be built. The deal had gone up in smoke, a potentially wonderful project that sadly had not turned into reality. With the turbulent relationships between Israel and the rest of the Arab world, Maurice's father was concerned that should the city be destroyed, it would cost a hell of a lot of money to rebuild. Nobody was willing to insure a city in such a volatile area, so the city remained a dream. Not even Lloyd's of London or the Israeli Government would commit to rebuilding the city, just like they would for any other city in Israel, if it was damaged during a war. In fact, the Finance Minister of Israel, himself, refused to promise that. This was the only tactical error Maurice's father made concerning the city, and it is only because of this, that the city never came to be.

At this point in my life, however, I was not convinced that Maurice would never again be part of my life. As it turned out, it wasn't too long until he was catapulted back into it—with tremendous force.

Part Four - After

Chapter Twenty-Nine

I got the news at work when Maurice called me. Shock was evident in his voice. "Garree, it's me. My father is dead. He was killed. I need to warn you that they're after me too."

His voice quivered dramatically at the mention of his father. "My father has been shot," he reported. I tried questioning him, but he responded by saying that he didn't know anything else at the moment. I crumpled to the floor, phone still in hand, completely numb. His father was a man whom I respected more than anyone else, and from whom I had managed to gain respect. Surprisingly, my first thoughts weren't of Maurice, but of his mother. I was scared for her. Had she been forced to witness the ordeal? How would she cope without her husband? I had so many questions running through my mind.

Then I thought of Maurice. How would he process his father's death? He admired his father, and I was sure he was putting on a brave façade on the phone with me. The call was heartbreaking. Moreover, I knew that "they" referred to the Iranian Government, which at this time was no longer ruled by the Shah but was instead led by Ayatollah Rabollek Komeinn and his religious fanatics who took over the country during the Iranian Revolution.

"Why?" I managed to choke out.

"They want our money. My father's money. The Revolutionary Guard have been dispatched to get me. I've gone into hiding, Garree. There's a million-dollar bounty on my head. If they find me, they'll torture me to get the family money. If they find out how close *we* were, they'll torture you to get to me. I'm going to travel the world and attend every sports event on the planet. I will never stop moving. Let them catch me if they can. So, this is goodbye, Garree. I love you. Don't worry."

Before I had time to respond, he hung up the phone. It took me a long while to process the words my friend had said. Gradually, through my grief, I began to make sense of the situation. To say the government in Iran had not been happy with Maurice's father would be an understatement. He was an outspoken advocate for Iran's Jewish population, and his work to support all those oppressed by the regime of the Shah was not viewed well by the current government. His opinions regarding the country, its oppression of the people, its corruption, and its inequality were beginning to become recognized by more and more people. Moreover, a revolution was brewing throughout the country and the government knew it. As a result of this, Maurice's father became a wanted man, and then they killed him. In truth, it was not a revolution for the people. Ali Khamenei's regime wanted to take the money and power the family had for themselves.

It was too much to process for me at the time. I simply accepted what I had been told—that Maurice's father was dead.

I was heartbroken that I lost contact with Maurice due to this incident, but as I have said before, life simply goes on. As time passed, I heard from various sources that Maurice was, in fact, traveling the world, and keeping safe. Mostly though, he remained a specter to me, lost in the mists of time and tragedy. Years passed, as they do.

Then, in 1993, out of the blue, Maurice showed up at my tire store. When he walked through the door, I felt like I'd seen a ghost. The Maurice I knew had not aged well. He had put on quite a bit of weight, his face was stoic, and his mannerisms were harder, more serious. That said, the young man standing next to him, was the spitting image of the twenty-year-old Maurice I remembered. When I see him in my thoughts or dreams, I never picture Maurice as an aged adult. He's still that twenty-year-old with the wry smile.

"Garree," he called to me. At least his voice had remained the same.

"Maurice!" I exclaimed, not sure whether to hug him, or put my hand through him to see if he was really there. I decided on a hug. "What are you doing here?" I asked, still completely taken aback as I let him go.

"I wanted to see if I could still find my way here."

"Oh, I'm sure that you'll never forget that."

"Actually, I'm taking my son to tour some colleges," he said. "Today we're visiting Brown University."

"I'm sure you'll like it," I told the young man. The university is in Providence, Rhode Island and is only ten miles away from my tire store. Then I turned my attention to Maurice. "Has everything been okay?" I asked, hinting at the elephant in the room.

"I'm alive, aren't I?" was his response. To me, it felt like a piece of the Maurice I remembered was shining through.

"Come in," I said. "Sit down. Let's catch up."

"I can't stay long," he replied, cryptically.

"Well come sit for a minute at least," I said. "I haven't seen you in years."

Maurice agreed, and, sitting down opposite me, began to proudly tell me about his new three-story warehouse in London, across the road from Big Ben. "No clocks or watches are allowed there, Garree," he said, that old Maurice grin appearing again on his face. "I spent about five million doing the place up. It's a gold mine! Come visit, Garree. It really has been far too long, old friend. I even built a room just for you and Ronna. You need to visit."

"I will, Maurice. If I can manage it."

Knowing he was about to leave, I looked him in the eye and said, "Let's travel through Europe again now that we're older but smarter."

"Garree," he countered, "we could never again catch lightning in the bottle like we did. We were on fire!"

I smiled. Maurice was still fast on his feet. In conversation, he could react faster than Muhammad Ali in the ring.

"Be glad we had such an experience once in our lifetime, as it really was special," he continued. "Let's be thankful we were together to share those experiences."

"You're right."

"Well," he said, standing up and looking at me intensely. "I've got to get going."

"Goodbye, Maurice."

"Goodbye, Garree."

I did not know then that this would be the last time I would ever see my best friend.

I intended to go and visit Maurice in London, but life got away from me. Five years later, in 1998, I got that phone call from Moritz that I described at the beginning of this book. Maurice died at the age of fifty-two. A massive heart attack got him. As I said, it was a mundane death that got him, way too soon, and one that Maurice would have despised. At least he died in his sleep. I know he would certainly have chosen to die on his feet, with a drink in his hand, his arm around a beautiful woman, and *Je T'aime* playing in the background.

After he died, I spent a lot of time reminiscing about my time with Maurice and the effect he had on me. When he walked into my tire store in 1993, my heart leapt to see my old friend, but I also thought to myself, "This is not the Maurice I know."

I honestly believe that I decided at some point that I did not want to see or know the older Maurice. I instead wanted to keep the mental image I had of the young man that I knew and loved. I wanted to only remember the one who could charm a snake, who could make you feel special, who had a class and breeding all of his own, who feared nothing, and loved life to the fullest. I wanted that version of Maurice untouched in my mind. He was such a figure in my imagination that, real or not, how I remembered my friend was extremely important to my sense of identity.

I have a confession to make. It depressed me when Maurice told me, "I wanted to see if I could still find my way here" after he walked into my tire shop that day in 1993. I needed my hero alive and well in my mind, charging through adventure after adventure across the world. He represented my youth and all the promise of those glittering days. As long as I kept the myth of that Maurice alive, I could also keep alive the myth of a young "Garree" for whom anything was possible. If the great Maurice could grow old and die, then what chance did *I* have? I would just be an old man in a tire shop. So, I refused to think of Maurice as anything other than a beautiful young man, still swaying under the lights and music of La Siesta with that grin of his planted on his face.

Shortly after he died, I read Maurice's obituary in *The Scribe* (a Journal of Babylonian Jewry). [1] I loved the way Victor, Maurice's best friend at the time, explained it all for I felt the exact same way.

MOISE ELGHANAYAN

Moise Elghanayan died very suddenly and unexpectedly in his sleep of a massive heart attack on the morning of Wednesday, March 11th, 1998, at the young age of fifty-two. He is survived by his loyal and dedicated wife, Rhonda, and his young son, David.

---

[1] Chitayat, Victor. "Moise Elghanayan." *The Scribe.* April 1998.

The peaceful manner in which Moise—Maurice to me—passed away contrasted sharply with the shock waves which were felt in communities around the world only hours after his death. The unexpected news had family, friends, and acquaintances reeling from the impact, in total disbelief. For here was a man loved by all, a doting father, a devoted husband, a wonderful friend to many, and a large benefactor to numerous charities, taken in such a tragic and untimely way. The burial took place at Edgwarebury Cemetery in London on a Friday and was attended by the largest group ever witnessed at the Cemetery. Family and friends flew from all corners of the globe to pay their last farewell to their dear friend. Rabbi Abraham Levy made a poignant address, expressing everyone's feelings about what an impact Moise had on everyone who came in contact with him, and how short his stay was on this Earth. He further went on to praise Moise for being such a dedicated son to his parents while they were alive. He explained that Moise was born in Iran, was the only son of Davoud and Aghdas Elghanayan, and that he was a very successful businessman with interests in many areas, renowned for spotting opportunities and for being a visionary. He said that his ideas and projects always seemed to be one or two steps ahead of others, and that everyone who worked with him trusted him implicitly. That his generosity and hospitality to friends and family were legendary. Further, the rabbi said that Moise had a phenomenal memory for numbers; and was a world class backgammon player. It is prophetic, the rabbi maintained, that he died on Erev Purim, the start of a Jewish holiday that, among other things, celebrates charity.

As the rabbi concluded:

Moise's life is a fascinating story, and as most stories,
we wish it would go on forever, but we understand that even

the best of stories have to end. So instead of grieving that it had to end, we should feel blessed that we were lucky enough to have been a part of it. So farewell, dear friend, may you rest in peace and know that you will be in our hearts forever. —**Victor Chitayat**

Chapter Thirty

I learned so much by having Maurice and his family be a part of my life. In fact, my life would have been so different had I never met the man—had I never seen that grin spread across his young face when he knew something I didn't. Even to this day, I can hear him say, "Always shoot for the stars. That way even if you land on the moon, you'll be way ahead of everyone else." Anytime those words pass through my mind, memories of Maurice and all that we experienced together swirl around me.

I like to believe that Maurice never opened up to anyone else the way he did to me on those long drives through Europe. I loved and respected the way he spoke about his close-knit, yet secretive family, with such deep love. I still feel privileged to have been welcomed by them. I firmly believe that I was the only non-Iranian American that had been allowed to bond with him and his family in such a way. After all, the only others outside the immediate family who were as close to him as I had become were Maurice's cousins. In any case, that's what I would like to believe. Of course, I can't be sure. As I said, they were secretive, and understandably so.

I've lived a normal happy life since Maurice passed away. Ronna and I have done the whole "white picket fence" thing, and I could not be more content. My son, Scott, and daughter, Kimberly, are both successful adults with families of their own. I bought the tire business from my father in 1986 for more than it was worth, and for fifty years, I got to do something I was good at and loved. I continued to be careful with my money and saved whatever I could. Because of that, I was able to retire in 2014, at the age of sixty-eight, and enjoy my new life as a grandfather.

Do I have any regrets? Sure. Who doesn't? I wish I had chosen Maurice to be the best man at my wedding, and really worked hard to make that happen. I wish I'd been able to go to his wedding in London. I wish we could have gotten to know each other's children and grandchildren. Aside from all that though, I'm glad that Maurice saw me as a giver, not as a taker. This taught me to be proud of my nature. If I had not been the only one that said "thank you" for the drinks he bought everyone during the spring break of 1965, my world would have been a much smaller place. Oh, how my life would have been different without him in it! Seeing Maurice do the impossible too many times to count, made me realize that *I* could do the impossible too. I think we can all learn to live a little bit more like Maurice, who, though far from perfect, was so unapologetically himself.

Everyone with whom I've shared some of Maurice's stories have told me to write a book about them. "The stories are unbelievable," they would say. So that's exactly what I did. I wrote this to honor him, to honor his family, and to honor all those affected by the topics covered in this book.

Perhaps you too have a Maurice in your life: a larger-than-life character that imprints on you early and forever. They may be gone, as Maurice is, but I like to think he's looking down on me, or maybe, in Maurice's case, looking *up!*

I can even picture him now, that big smile spreading across his face, saying "Don't worry Garree. You did a great job!" Living life to the fullest was what Maurice was all about. By sharing his story with the world, I feel like I'm celebrating that vibrant man, my dearest friend and mentor, in the way he so richly deserves. He was truly one in a billion.

Epilogue

The Search for the Truth

As the years passed, the desire to share my life stories with my family started to grow. And when I did, I was told by them that I should write a book. As such, I decided to write it in the form of a memoir, which I embarked on after I retired in 2014. And so, I began looking into the past (as one does when writing their memoirs), and as I did, I realized I had more questions than answers regarding the events that led to the death of Maurice's father, Davoud.

I became obsessed with finding out the truth, or as much of the truth as I could, and it took me years to piece the information together required to write this book in its entirety. Eventually, I found an article[2] on Israeled.org—the online publication of the Center for Israeli Education (CIE)—which gave me pause. Wasn't it Maurice's father Davoud, not his uncle Habib, who had been killed by the Iranian regime? I read on, breathlessly intrigued. Here is that online article, in its entirety:

---

[2] Israeled.org. "Iranian Jewish Leader Habib Elghanian is Executed." May 9ᵗʰ, 1979. https://israeled.org/iranian-jewish-leader-habib-elghanian-executed/

May 9, 1979

Born in Tehran in 1912, Habib Elghanian became a prominent Iranian businessman, importing a variety of consumer goods into Iran, including watches, electronics, textiles, and clothing. By the conclusion of World War II, Elghanian and his partners had made over one million.

Following the war, Elghanian branched out into the production of plastic goods, beginning with a single molding machine in 1948. His company, Plasco, would become the largest plastics manufacturer in the Middle East. Elghanian brought the latest technologies to his business which he continued to expand into areas such as appliance manufacturing, mining, and textiles.

He was elected chairman of the Jewish community in 1959. Together with his brother, Davoud, and other Iranian Jewish businessmen, Elghanian organized a charitable association which provided needed funds for the health and welfare of Iran's poor Jews, including medical services and a school meals program. Elghanian's charitable work was not limited to the Jewish community; he donated his first home to be turned into a hospital.

Elghanian was a frequent visitor to and investor in Israel. In 1968, he and his brothers built the Shimshon Tower in Tel-Aviv and purchased the Tehran home that would become the Israeli Embassy in Iran. When popular protests against the Shah intensified in the fall of 1978, Elghanian was in the United States on business. Although he was urged by friends and family not to return to a now volatile Iran, Elghanian felt he had nothing to fear. He returned to Tehran in early 1979, stopping in Israel on the way. He was arrested on March 16. After being held for nearly two months, Elghanian was put on trial on May 8. The brief show trial lasted only twenty minutes and Elghanian was convicted of being a Zionist spy and a "corrupter on Earth." He was sentenced to death by firing squad.

On May 9, 1979, Elghanian was executed.

His execution will heighten the anxiety of Iranian Jews and will expedite the Jewish exodus from Iran that started after the Islamic Revolution.

Reading the article above made my head spin. I had to check other newspapers to confirm the information. When various newspapers (the New York Times, The London Times, The Jerusalem Post, and a few others) printed the story of an Iranian businessman's assassination—the first civilian assassination by a revolutionary firing squad—they never mentioned Maurice's father's name, Davoud. Instead, they referred to the assassinated individual as Habib, which was Maurice's uncle's name. Many different reasons for this apparent discrepancy swam around my head when I was researching this. Perhaps they had gotten the name wrong? There were six brothers after all. Perhaps they had killed the wrong man? Maybe it was all an elaborate story created by the Islamic Revolution to scare the remaining Iranian Jews? If it was actually any of those options, other questions would need to be answered. For instance, why would Maurice tell me that his father had died if it was, in fact, his uncle? I just didn't understand why he would lie to me. I was hurt that he didn't trust me enough to tell me the whole story. Then again, I wondered if I was making this whole thing into something it was not. Maybe it was as simple as the newspapers getting the name wrong.

To try and understand what had actually happened, I sent letters out to

Maurice's family, inquiring about these unusual circumstances. I reasoned that since the danger had passed as had many years, someone might be able to help me unlock the secrets of this mystery.

Responses to the letters I had sent out to Maurice's family were few and far between. Most seemed to not want to tell me what had happened. Even so, the questions I had clawed around in my brain, eating away at me. I did all I could do and waited impatiently for everyone I contacted to get back to me. Though the responses came in dribs and drabs, the ones I did get (mostly tidbits of hearsay) intrigued me even more. Some of them actually hinted that Maurice's father was still alive. As such, I knew I had to dig deeper.

Between various newspaper articles I found detailing Habib's death, and my sporadic conversations with the members of Maurice's family who would speak with me, I did ultimately manage to piece together the real truth. I was especially fortunate to have been called at work by somebody who claimed to know the entire story, due to having inside information. This obviously piqued my interest, even more so when he claimed to have the transcript of Habib's trial, and in its entirety I might add.

He did, however, ask for an exorbitant amount of money for this information. Though it was an amount that Maurice would have easily been able to part with, I could not do so. We ended up agreeing on a price for a list of Habib's charges. Even this, however, was more money than I felt comfortable parting with, but I just couldn't let it go. I felt compelled to find out more, much to my wife's disappointment. Ronna, as it turned out, was a huge support throughout my crazed journey to find information concerning Habib's death, but I could tell she'd rather I focus on our family. That said, the story I uncovered was, for me, too fascinating to turn away from.

As it turned out, it was not Maurice's father who was executed, it *was* Maurice's uncle Habib. You see, it was Habib who was the face of the company, which he owned with Maurice's father and his three other brothers.

It would make sense that Davoud, too, was a wanted man, given that the new Iranian regime wanted information concerning the money the family had invested overseas. As such, it made sense that Habib would be the primary target. A brave man until the very end, he wasn't one to hide his face in order to live quietly. He was the life and soul of the family and Maurice's idol. Maurice admired his father but very much looked up to his uncle.

When Habib heard that he was a wanted man in the eyes of the Islamic Revolution, he went straight to Switzerland and did two things: he wrote out his will and spent ten full days preparing his defense by writing down all of the good things he had done for the country, hoping it would make a difference in the eyes of his biased future captors. After all, he employed over one million Iranians and brought Iran into the Industrial Age. Knowing the kind of battle he was about to face, he also prepared for the eventuality of his death. He was under no misconceptions of what would be waiting for him when he returned to Iran. As such, Habib instructed Maurice to take a copy of his updated will to the World Court should anything happen to him, believing that this was the only way his wishes would be carried out fairly. The World Court is the principal Judicial organ of the United Nations and is located within Hague, in the Netherlands. This court is responsible for settling international legal disputes, which Habib's money certainly was. When Habib updated his will, he ensured that his money was hidden in safety deposit boxes in London, Switzerland, and Turkey so as to keep it away from the Revolutionary Guard and the Ayatollah, who believed they were entitled to it.

I believe Maurice's father helped him with this, transferring Habib's assets through the Israeli Diamond Exchange. In so doing, the assets would be readily available for Davoud's close family to utilize. Maurice's father was known by family and friends as "The Accountant" since he had the ways and means to transfer money and assets without getting caught.

Maurice's father had hidden the family's fortune in various bank accounts, businesses, and properties across the world, under different spellings of the family's last name, just in case the Shah's regime fell. The majority of Davoud's cash was hidden in the United Kingdom. Their ultimate destination was London, a much more secure place to stash millions. He was a man who knew how to plan ahead, after all.

I believe that when Habib decided to face his opposition, he hoped they would see reason and allow him and his family to be free. When I spoke to Karmel, Habib's son who had once dated my younger sister (born in 1950), he explained that Habib believed he was going to deal with "normal, rational people." He couldn't have been more mistaken.

Upon landing in Tehran, Habib was arrested by the Islamic Revolutionary Guard and taken straight to jail. The charges against him included being a friend of God's enemy (Israel), being a spy, and being a capitalist. All these charges were seen by Iranian officials as the worst crimes you could possibly commit and was evidenced in his treatment. He was not even allowed to return to his home before being imprisoned.

During Habib's imprisonment, his head was shaved in order to humiliate him, and he was only allowed the occasional visitor, food, and water. The severity of his situation became even more apparent when a family friend visited Habib in prison. They met in a bare, stone room, Habib's prison clothes trailing on the floor behind him. Keeping his head high, he greeted his old friend, showing all who were watching that he was not a broken man. The friend promised Habib that he would help make sure his children got the money they were entitled to if he would tell him where all of the money and assets were hidden. Habib saw straight through the smoke and mirrors. His old friend was being threatened, more than likely with the death and torture of his family, so that the Islamic Revolutionary Guard could get their hands on his fortune. Having no choice but to tell him that he was unable to do what he asked, Habib turned around and walked back to his cell, alone again.

It is rumored that the Mossad had a plan to break him out of prison, something Habib refused. He didn't want to lead a life on the run. He wanted to face those who hunted him head-on like the courageous man he was, and not run like a coward, always looking over his shoulder.

Habib's old friend returned a week or so later to beg for Habib's forgiveness for what he had tried to do. He explained that the Revolutionary Guard, the enforcers of the new Iranian regime, had a plan to break him, and that they were determined to get his money, which they believed to be rightfully theirs. Habib's old friend then told him that he could leave and never return to Iran if he told the Revolutionary Guard where his money was. Habib must have considered the offer, as any man would. In the end, however, Habib allegedly said, "I am not leaving my country. I am not leaving my people. I will not be buried in a foreign land. If I am to die, let me die like a man, defending my honor and standing up for what I believe." He was killed shortly afterward.

Habib was shot by a firing squad on May 9, 1979, a matter of hours after his conviction before the "Supreme Leader," Ayatollah Ruhollah Khomeini. It has also been suggested by some that Khomeini needed Habib and his family out of the way. The regime could not risk having such high-profile, rich, and well-liked people speaking out against it. Unfortunately, the easiest way to do this, and to get their hands on a vast amount of money, was to accuse the family of crimes and have their "ringleader" executed. As an added benefit, this would send a message to the entire Iranian Jewish population to "get out and leave both their possessions and wealth behind."

After even more years of research, I found an article on Ancestry.com which helped me conclude that Maurice's father, Davoud, had died in London (under the name Davod), not too far from where his daughter Flora had lived all those years ago. In fact, the article not only included the correct date of birth, but it also included Maurice's mother's name, Aghdas. Both of these solidified, in my mind, that the article was actually about Maurice's father. Either way, what I had found out was that when Habib was killed, Maurice's father had gone into hiding. I believe he had a contingency plan to fake his death so that he would not have to look over his shoulder for the rest of his life. I also believe that he purchased two dead bodies from the morgue, burnt his house to the ground, and had his brother, who was previously a colonel in the Iranian Air Force, fly him and his wife to Turkey in the helicopter he always kept on the roof. Given that there were no CSIs in Iran at the time, no investigation into the dead bodies were launched. As such, the reports in Iranian newspapers explaining that Davoud and his wife were shot before the house was burned down (which was how I learned of this) was simply accepted by everyone. I honestly do not think Maurice knew his mother was alive, or that the house had burned down when he told me his father had been shot. I believe he just heard that his father was shot and that he should be careful. The Iranian Revolutionary Guard (more commonly known as the Revolutionary Guard) were after the family fortune and would stop at nothing to get to it. Davoud knew that his country was not stable and would eventually become hostile toward him so I think he took the opportunity to run. After all, he was an Israeli sympathizer, and in the eyes of the Iranian Revolutionary Guard, nothing was worse than that.

It was suggested in some reports that Maurice's father had links with the Mossad, and that it was that link that enabled him to leave the country without a trace as quickly and as easily as he did. The passport Maurice's father left the country with was real, however. There was no doubt about that. That said, by changing Davoud to Davod, and changing Elghanayan to Elghanian, a new person was born. Unlike his brother, Maurice's father got to live the rest of his life in peace, though it must have been a far simpler life than he was accustomed to. That is to say, there would be no more homes fashioned after casinos. No more state meetings. No more

100 suitcases delivered to his house. But that no longer mattered. He escaped with his life.

If I knew Maurice's father at all, I knew he would have adapted to his new life without any difficulties. He was always one to make lemonade from lemons, after all. He cared about his family and the good of humanity over anything else. I believe he lived a life where those things were in abundance. Interestingly, Flora claims to this day that she did not know her father was in England, and I believe her. She was never one to lie. Plus, it is more than likely that Davoud told no one where he was hidden, not even Maurice or Flora, in order to keep everybody safe.

I found an article in the early 2000s that said Maurice's father escaped to Turkey via his helicopter flown by his brother who had been a Colonel in the Iranian air force. He had apparently been planning his escape for a long time. He had hidden massive amounts of cash in Turkey which helped him make it to London with his wife, completely unharmed. I can only speculate that he bribed an official to change the name on his passport so he couldn't be tracked. The reason for my suspicions is that I learned of his death on a website where you can track family histories. I found a record of the death of a man, who just so happened to have Maurice's father's date of birth but had one letter different in his first name. This matched up with what I was told by Karmel when I had spoken to him. He said that the family had known of his escape through Turkey, but that was it. The cousin agreed that Maurice's father would have bribed officials to change their passports. He also agreed that it was definitely Maurice's father's obituary I had found.

By rights I should have been happy that I had located Maurice's father and pieced together what had happened to him and his wife, but I wasn't. I simply couldn't imagine what Maurice's mother and father had experienced when fleeing the country. To leave their children behind and then lead them to believe that their father and mother was dead must have been torture for the once close family. Nevertheless, I was sure that Maurice's mother and father had settled down and lived the rest of their lives in a small Jewish community in London. After all, if they had gone to an Iranian community, the Revolutionary Guard may have found them. I also feel that they would have been happy there, all things considered, because they had each other.

Habib, the man who died at the hands of the Islamic Revolution, has gone down in history. His death is remembered to this day by many people, and not only by those who are Jewish, Iranian, or Israeli. His death—the first civilian execution—caused ripples across the world. That said, as I sit in front of my computer writing this story, Iran is back in the news. The Supreme Leader of Iran, Ali Khamenei, seems ready to start the second phase of his Islamic Revolution, that is to say, the capture of wealth from the people they deem to be enemies of the state. Furthermore, the attitude of Iranian leaders toward Israel still seems to be the same as it was during the first revolution—the one that led to Habib's death and caused Maurice and his family to go into hiding.

The family's plight, however, did not end with the death of Habib, as he would have more than likely wished. His children, for instance, defended Habib's will against the Iranian Government and wanted all the money invested outside of Iran (whether they be in companies, or properties) to be included, money that would normally be turned over to the Iranian Government who had killed Habib. After a long and arduous battle, the U.S. courts decided that they had no jurisdiction over the Iranian money hidden in the U.S., and that was that. Nonetheless, his children, nieces, and nephews were well looked after. It had been arranged, prior to Habib's death, for them to all have a share of the *family* wealth (all the assets found outside of Iran). This was done quietly and under the radar with the help of Maurice's father. Although the family would be worried about their personal futures, the last thing Habib wanted was for the Guard to be aware of how the money was distributed, which would have made his family an even larger target.

However, the family's battle over Habib's money had not quite ended, as the fight over Habib's money was still ongoing at the World Court. After a decade-long battle, the World Court decided in favor of the family and not the Iranian Government. Little did anyone know that the Iranian Government was only fighting for a portion of the money. As previously stated, a large portion of money was hidden in land, buildings, businesses all over the world, and all under different names! For example, over $3.5 billion dollars was hidden in U.S. real estate and businesses alone! This was his final rebellion against those oppressing him. I guess he had the last laugh. Still, in a raid of Habib's home right after his death, $155 million worth of jewelry, cash and gold was found, assets it seemed he hadn't quite got around to selling off.

The sad fact of it is, the Iranian Government was threatened by the family's prowess and their ability to make change. Imagine, if Maurice's father had been able to build his city, how much better off the Iranian Jews would have been. They would be safer, and the history of the 75,000 Iranian Jews in particular would have been very different.

The story behind this book, the trials and tribulations of Iran, and how one family coped with it, was just as important to me as telling Maurice's story. I think it's important to know what's going on in the world around you and remember to never judge a book by its cover. Looking at Maurice's family, given their wealth, you might have had the impression that they thought they were worth more than everyone else. Dig a little deeper though, and you discover that they had hearts as big as their bank accounts.

• • •

In this book you have met many people. Some may have only been part of the story for a little while. Nevertheless, the part they played was important. After the roles they played in mine and Maurice's story I think it's only fair that you know what happened to them.

Flora

Flora became the queen of London society after partnering with David Shamoon in nightclubs and casinos. However, when her husband was arrested due to being part of the largest case of fraud ever recorded on the London Stock Exchange, she divorced him. Later, she married her Italian personal trainer, sold her share of the business she had partnered with David to run, moved to a huge villa in Italy, and lived there for ten years or so. She wanted to make sure the Revolutionary Guard couldn't find her, and she wanted her own peace of mind. That said, missing the spotlight and glamour of London, she eventually returned and opened another very successful business, on her own this time. She had her father's business sense and has remained the classiest woman I've ever had the pleasure of meeting. Flora has achieved what she set out to do and made a fortune. Flora and David, furthermore, had helped start the careers of many famous artists, including The Beatles, Elton John, and The Rolling Stones. Their club, The Speakeasy, was the place to be for hip young artists. I personally think Flora could have bought every house on the Street with No Name and still had money left over when she came back from Italy.

I will always have a soft spot for Flora. She was the first woman who showed me what class and elegance truly was. She wanted to prove her worth, but she was never in competition with her father.

David Shamoon

David, much like Flora, achieved everything he set out to do. He lived the life of a celebrity, rubbing elbows with the elite, the rich, and the famous.

215

Needless to say, given that both David and Flora were business partners, David was equally instrumental in launching many a music career. His clubs, furthermore, remained in high demand with celebrities from all over the world. For twenty years, he rode high on the London scene—until he was investigated and found guilty of consorting with the London Mob. He ended up spending time in prison. It is important to note that Flora had sold her share of their business before this happened. Regardless of this ending, I'll bet that if you asked David if he would be willing to trade lives with someone else, he would say no. After all, he achieved his dreams, and rose to the top without the help of his father who offered to give him one third of his estate when he was on his deathbed. David refused in no uncertain terms; he didn't need the money. Both David and Flora honored their handshake until Flora left the country.

Maurice's Father (Davoud)

As related earlier, he was known as "The Accountant." It has been said that he was the smartest of all the brothers, which could be true. Davoud and his wife escaped the Islamic Revolution, with the help of his brother, who flew them to Turkey. He lived his remaining years quietly, with his wife by his side, unbeknownst to anyone.

Melina

Melina went on to become the head of the IT department at the largest bank in Massachusetts. While working there, she met her husband, a real-estate developer, had children, and remained happily married. At least I was responsible for something good, since she came to the U.S. because of me. She was a fantastic addition to the country, and I feel proud to have had a hand in that.

Moritz

I caught up with Moritz not too long ago. Sadly, his dad died and left him out of his will. I got the impression that Moritz was a deeply unhappy man. I offered him a ticket to the U.S., but he refused to take it. Not long after, his email address stopped working and I was unable to contact him. I have no idea what happened to him. I fear for the worst but hope for the best.

Flora's Maid

Flora's maid stayed by Flora's side until the very end. She went to Italy with Flora and returned to London with her too. In fact, she happily remained with Flora until her death a few years ago.

Flora's Daughter

Much like Maurice, she went to the best boarding schools in the world. A trust was set up for her by both Flora and Davoud, her grandfather. She too had to go underground as a result of her family's complication, but it was much easier for her than for others. She didn't know much about the family business, after all. I'm not sure where she is today, but I'd wager that whatever she's doing, she is probably unbelievably successful, just like her mother

My Father and My Mother

My relationship with my father always remained strained. He had two entirely different sides: one day he would act like your best friend, and the next he might stab you in the back just to prove he was better than you. I loved the good side of my dad but hated the bad. He died of lung cancer at sixty-eight and argued with me until his very last day. He was a tyrant to me and even left me out of his will, though what hurt me much more was seeing the way he treated my mother. She was old-fashioned, had only ever been with my father, and didn't know any different. My mother had a heart of gold, but she never stood up for herself when it came to my father. She died when she was eighty-six, outliving my father by fifteen years.

Maurice's Uncles

I related that Maurice's father had five brothers—Maurice's uncle John lived out his life quietly in New York City investing a fortune in U.S. real estate. Uncle Habib has played a considerable part in our story, but what about the other brothers? One of them lived out his life quietly, running the Israeli Diamond Exchange. The mechanical genius who was a colonel in the Iranian Air Force flew Davoud and wife to Turkey (as previously stated) and chose to stay there afterwards. He then opened a very successful repair shop. That said, the jailed brother, the one who needed to be bailed out for Flora's wedding, continued on the same path as he always had.

The Shah of Iran

The last Persian Monarch, the Shah was exiled to Egypt on January 16, 1979. He died while in exile in July, 1980 of non-Hodgkin lymphoma. He died a broken man, having been stripped of his status. I still believe he wasn't a bad man, just weak. While the extent of the Shah's wealth is unknown, some suggest his estimated total wealth was somewhere in the region of $100 million. It is interesting to note here that Khamenei, the current leader of Iran, is worth approximately $95 billion, all of which was stolen from the Iranian people. Read into that what you will.

The Empress Soraya

It is said that the Shah loved his first wife until the day he died. One of the most glamorous women of her day, she became Empress of Iran at the age sixteen, but was repudiated by her husband seven years later since she was unable to bear him an heir to the peacock throne. Due to her giving personality, Soraya became the most loved and cherished person in all of Europe. Her humanitarian work is the stuff of legends. She was held in high esteem in Europe in the same way as the Kennedys were in the United States, a fact that made her untouchable by the Revolutionary Guard. Soraya died in Paris of natural causes at the age of sixty-nine.

The Empress Farah

Also known as "Her Imperial Princess," she married the Shah in 1959 and remained married to him until his death. Remember the nine dresses Flora made for her? She lived a high maintenance lifestyle when married to the Shah. That said, she now lives a very quiet, anonymous life in the U.S. due to her fear of retaliation by the Revolutionary Guard.

Maurice

Definitely, the one and only. My dear friend was never able to live up to his own expectations, but not for lack of trying. In my opinion he never found his center—that one thing that would have given him purpose. Still, I can personally attest to the fact that Maurice lived his life to the fullest. While he called me one in a million, he always remained one in a billion to me. I only wish he was here to read this book.

La Siesta

To me, there never was nor never will be another La Siesta as it did have the class, character, and elegance it advertised. It was above and beyond any place I ever attended. It's the only place that I visited time and time again, and yet it never diminished my love for it. Somehow, I found myself in that one-of-a-kind place. Sadly, just like 1968, it no longer exists . It was knocked down and became a poor man's casino—right after the owners all died.

Photographs from Gary's Personal Collection

The night before we left for Europe—
Joined by Maurice's cousin, Karmal. 1968.

Maurice at the Blarney Castle with not a worry in the world. 1968.

Gary with the maid Mina and Flora's daughter in front of Flora's home on the Street with No Name and the House with No Number. 1968.

Flora with Maurice—Smashing brother and sister. 1968.

Dachau—An unforgettable experience. 1968.

Celebrating July 4th at the Hofbräuhaus House in Germany. 1968.

After Gary had changed the tire, Maurice insisted that Gary take a photo of him posing in this way. Maurice wanted to show this photograph to his dad. This proves his sleight of hand, does it not? 1968.

Maurice dressed to kill for a night out in the South of France. 1968.

The famous La Siesta bats. 1968.

The Pool You Dance on along with the Rowboat to Rescue any Patron that
"Happens to Fall In." 1968.

When you travel with Maurice, you really can dance on water. 1968.

Gary and Maurice's mother at La Siesta. 1968.

Gary receiving a ticket on Maurice's behalf. 1968.

Gary and Maurice, still brothers after spending sixty days and sixty nights together. 1969.

Gary and Melina hitching a ride to Woodstock along with sixteen others. 1969.

Gary and Melina at Woodstock—Spent three days and two nights right there. 1969.

The gang all together—Celebrating life. 1969.

Pick "A" (Andrea) or "B" (Ronna)—I Picked B. 1970.

Gary and Ronna dancing on water at La Siesta—A promise kept. 1973.

Bibliography

Bahari, Maziar and Roland Elliot Brown. "A Proud Jewish Iranian Killed by the Islamic Government." *IranWire*. February 8, 2017. https://iranwire.com/en/features/4343.

Chitayat, Victor. "Moise Elghanayan." *The Scribe*. April 1998.

Elghanayan v. Elghanayan. 148 Misc. 2d 552. (N.Y. Sup. Ct. 1990.)

Encyclopedia Iranica. "Elqāniān, Ḥabib." Last modified February 5, 2013. https://www.iranicaonline.org/articles/elqanian-habib.

Geni.com. "Davoud Elghanayan (Elghanian)." Last modified May 24, 2018. https://www.geni.com/people/Davoud-lghanayan/6000000050956904886.

Israeled.org. "Iranian Jewish Leader Habib Elghanian is Executed." May 9, 1979. https://israeled.org/iranian-jewish-leader-habib-elghanian-executed/

Melamed, Karmel. "Escape, Exile, Rebirth: Iranian Jewish Diaspora Alive and Well in Los Angeles." *Jewish Journal*. September 4, 2008. https://jewishjournal.com/community/65726/escape-exile-rebirth-iranian-jewish-diaspora-alive-and-well-in-los-angeles/.

Wikipedia. "Habib Elghanian." Last modified November 17, 2020. https://en.wikipedia.org/wiki/Habib_Elgahanian.